# Facilitating Change

Ready-to-use training materials for the manager

# Facilitating Change

Ready-to-use training materials for the manager

Barry Fletcher

Gower

© Barry Fletcher 1997

The materials that appear in this book, other than those quoted from prior sources, may be reproduced for education/training activities. There is no requirement to obtain special permission for such uses.

This permission statement is limited to reproduction of materials for educational or training events. Systematic or large-scale reproduction or distribution – or inclusion of items in publication for sale – may be carried out only with prior written permission from the publisher.

Published by
Gower Publishing Limited
Gower House
Croft Road
Aldershot
Hampshire GU11 3HR
England

Gower Publishing Limited
Old Post Road
Brookfield
Vermont 05036
USA

Barry Fletcher has asserted his right under the Copyright, Designs and Patents Act 1988 to be identified as the author of this work.

British Library Cataloguing in Publication Data
Fletcher, Barry, 1943–
    Facilitating change: ready-to-use training materials for the manager
    1. Organizational change
    I. Title
    658.4'06

ISBN 0 566 07662 4

Library of Congress Cataloging-in-Publication Data
Fletcher, Barry.
    Facilitating change: ready-to-use training materials for the
  manager / Barry Fletcher.
      p.  cm.
    Includes index.
    ISBN 0-566-07662-4 (cloth)
    1. Organizational change—Study and teaching—Activity programs.
  2. Organizational learning—Study and teaching—Activity programs.
I. Title.
HD58.8.F548   1997
658.4'06'07155—DC20                                                96–41363
                                                                                               CIP

Typeset in Great Britain by Bournemouth Colour Press Limited, Parkstone, Dorset and printed in Great Britain at the University Press, Cambridge.

# Contents

| | |
|---|---|
| Preface | vii |
| Acknowledgements | ix |
| Introduction | 1 |

**Part I  Helping your staff to learn**

**1  Management, learning and the management of learning** — **11**
 A recap on managing — 11
 A recap on learning — 13
 Feedback — 14
 A closer look at learning — 15
 Learning about learning — 15
 The parts people play — 16
 Linking managing to learning — 16

**2  Getting to grips with staff development** — **19**
 Training and learning — 20
 Where do you stand on staff development? — 21
 Determining your role — 23
 Understanding the context — 23
 Organizational learning culture — 25

**3  Diagnosing needs and recognizing opportunities** — **27**
 Determining the needs of your staff — 27
 Indicators of learning and development needs — 28
 Skilful questioning — 28
 The use of commentary — 32
 The rewards of 'active listening' — 33
 Opportunities for learning — 34
 Recognizing what has worked well — 35

**4  Confirming the need and contracting the action** — **37**
 Contracting the learning — 38

| | | |
|---|---|---|
| 5 | **Using closed-circuit television** | **41** |
| 6 | **Collaborating with others** | **45** |
| 7 | **Review, evaluation and maintaining momentum** | **47** |
| | Review and evaluation questionnaire | 47 |
| | Maintaining momentum | 48 |

## Part II  The activities

| | | |
|---|---|---|
| | Index to activities | 51 |
| | Time checklist | 55 |
| | Individual group use | 57 |
| | *The activities* | |
| 1 | Raising my awareness of me | 59 |
| 2 | Heightening my awareness of my values | 63 |
| 3 | Reordering my personal goals | 67 |
| 4 | Increasing my creativity | 79 |
| 5 | Raising my confidence | 83 |
| 6 | Improving my listening | 87 |
| 7 | Overcoming resistance to situations I avoid | 91 |
| 8 | Reducing my self-doubts | 95 |
| 9 | Letting go of my old behaviours | 101 |
| 10 | Widening my support network | 111 |
| 11 | Strengthening my motivation | 119 |
| 12 | Reducing harmful stress | 127 |
| 13 | Making loss a new beginning | 135 |
| 14 | Adjusting to the phases of transition | 141 |
| 15 | Lessening the pain of change | 147 |
| 16 | Raising awareness of the value of people | 151 |
| 17 | Discovering ways of helping and influencing others | 157 |
| 18 | Triggering my ability to influence others | 163 |
| 19 | Discovering new ways to learn | 167 |
| 20 | Removing the blinkers | 175 |
| 21 | Understanding reactions to change | 185 |
| 22 | Identifying strategies for change | 199 |
| 23 | Discovering key organizational goals | 215 |
| 24 | Developing team goals | 223 |
| 25 | Introducing change at work | 231 |
| 26 | Striving for internal quality | 237 |
| 27 | Introducing new patterns of work | 245 |
| 28 | Creating customer-conscious attitudes | 253 |
| 29 | Shifting our attitudes to service | 263 |
| 30 | Improving customer care | 269 |
| 31 | Increasing customer markets | 279 |
| 32 | Empowering others | 287 |
| 33 | Providing a challenge | 291 |
| 34 | Taking a risk | 293 |
| 35 | Welcoming the unknown | 297 |

# Preface

Change is here to stay. I've been in the change business for most of my working life as a manager, trainer, facilitator and consultant. Often I've been invited to help people and organizations with the changes they are instigating or having to make.

For several years my business was training; presenting courses, putting on a performance and generally doing to trainees those things which other people, usually their managers, had decided would be good for them. I had some enjoyable times and I do believe that there were some benefits to trainees from the work I did. However, I used to question the value of training and what had happened after the event. For example, did people behave any differently? Did they feel more confident or competent? Had they learned anything new and of value to them?

I made a successful transition from the training to the learning business in the 1980s. How was this different and what had changed? The main change was in my own view of the world in so far as training and learning were concerned. I had realized that training is something *done to others* whereas learning is something *done by others for themselves*. Since then my work has taken on a different shape, with a degree of challenge being offered to those who think they know what's best for their staff. I encourage greater engagement with learners: first, engaging with them as people by listening, empathizing, showing interest and working to understand the fears, delights, concerns, successes, aspirations and disappointments within their world; second, engaging and working with them as enthusiastic learners, using my skills to help them prepare for, and face, what they have identified as life's new challenges.

In 1992 Gower published a resource manual *50 Activities for Achieving Change*, written by myself in conjunction with Ann Bell, Mike Whittaker and John Buttery. In it we presented 50 learning activities, based on the theme of change, for use by training professionals. In the course of writing that first manual I realized that much of the material, suitably adapted, would provide a valuable resource for managers.

The present manual, written for managers, is the outcome of that realization. It is written for managers because they, more than any other group, have the potential to facilitate the learning and continuous development of their staff. Whether they hold the title manager, supervisor, team leader or director, the term manager is used throughout this manual to refer to people who fulfil any and all of these roles.

This manual is designed to help you to help your staff achieve results, in terms of the quantity and quality of output which your internal and external customers require in order to remain committed to doing business with you. It is concerned with managing the changes which are necessary, and with creating conditions for new thoughts and actions to emerge. The emphasis is on promoting a climate, an atmosphere, a culture in which staff thirst for new knowledge, skills and approaches so that challenges, including competition, can be faced with confidence.

At the heart of this manual is a collection of learning activities. They can be used on their own or as part of a wider programme of learning and development. Their function is to help people to learn by guiding them through a number of carefully defined stages. Each activity consists of a brief description, a note of the expected benefits and who it is suitable for, which could be your staff, yourself or others. Also included are the steps to be taken and the time, resources and materials required.

Within the activities most of the planning and preparation has already been done for you. This leaves you free to concentrate on choosing appropriate activities and briefing people on their use, offering support during the activities and helping people to identify, and take decisions on applying their learning.

Since this is a manual about change, feel free to change and adapt it to your own needs and select from it what appeals to you. Above all, keep an open mind when using the activities, be willing to learn from them and also be prepared to change!

Barry Fletcher

# Acknowledgements

**My heartfelt thanks go to:**

Joan Fletcher and Anita Fletcher without whose direct help and unstinting support this manual would never have been written.

**Special thanks to:**

Paul O'Mahony for his numerous contributions, encouragement and sticking with me to the very end of the journey. Malcolm Stern of Gower for his patience and understanding.

**Thanks also to:**

Mark Fletcher, Tony Hogan, Sherran Hodkinson, Phil Balls, Chris Blantern, Rita McCormack, Mike Glossop, Dave Bundy, Pam Walton, Matthew Ramsden, David Walton, David Megginson, Tom Richardson, Ian Flemming, Pam Horner, Mike Whittaker, Debbie McKeith, Geoff Middleton, Alan Moore, Ellie Middleton, Rosalyn Barber, Pat Daley, Vince King, Wendy Flemming and Jan O'Mahony for their interest, support and inspiration, and the many people not mentioned above who have also 'done their bit' towards helping me become the person I am.

BF

# Introduction

There is no doubt that change is here to stay.

McCarthy* speaks of 'the immanence of change – change does not happen, it is happening constantly'.

A few minutes' reflection will confirm that nothing stands still. As a manager you will be no stranger to the changing environment. Typical changes which you have managed, coped with, responded to or initiated could include:

- taking on new staff
- forming a new team
- reorganization and restructuring
- amalgamation, takeover, acquisition, redundancy
- new technology
- new working methods
- legislation
- losing old customers and acquiring new ones
- increasing productivity and efficiency
- raising effectiveness
- career progression
- developing new products and services
- training and developing others.

---

*McCarthy, M: 'Ancient wisdom: new science – towards a philosophy of change', *Management Education and Development*, Vol 21, Part 1, 1990.

The people with whom you interact are also involved in change, in their work and in their lives generally. Furthermore, you will probably have recognized your key role in helping your staff to initiate, accommodate, sustain and benefit from change.

This manual is designed to help you to concentrate on this challenging, change-enabling aspect of your work. It contains some key concepts, simply described, a number of stand-alone activities for you to use as a resource, and some practical suggestions for achieving change.

Chapter 1 encourages you to reflect on the subjects of management and learning and shows how to link them together in your everyday work as a manager. Chapter 2 invites you to explore your stance and role in relation to learning and development. The remaining chapters in Part I take you step by step through a process for diagnosing and taking action on the learning and development needs of your staff within the framework of change. The learning activities in Part II are intended as a resource for you to facilitate the learning of your staff, and possibly yourself, thereby bringing about change.

The rest of this introduction contains a few more words about change and learning as a context for the remainder of the manual.

## Background to change

There is much mythology about change! Many of us have been brought up to distrust it, to treat it with caution, even to avoid it. Of course some changes can be painful – but so can life. Other people seem to welcome change; indeed, they actively seek it out and recognize the opportunities it brings.

We are surrounded by change. Think about some obvious examples: bereavement; changing jobs, systems and procedures; changing friendships and relationships; growing older; moving from infant to child to adolescent to adult; becoming a parent.

So why does one individual accept or welcome change whereas another will resist or reject it? Studying the comments given below may offer some answers to this question.

*I might accept or welcome change because:*

- my personal security is increased
- I anticipate more opportunities to use my skills
- my salary will be increased
- the new situation offers me more job satisfaction
- I will have more responsibility

*Introduction*

- my working conditions will be improved
- the new situation will save me time and require less effort
- I will be facing new challenges
- my status will be raised
- my career prospects will be increased
- I feel I am set in my ways
- I am becoming bored and starting to stagnate
- my ideas have been listened to
- I trust the people who want to make the change
- I believe we must move forward
- we cannot afford to stand still
- this gives me the opportunity to show what I can do
- I've been kept fully in the picture.

*I might resist or reject change because:*

- I don't know why they want to change things
- I like the way things are
- I'm too old to change
- it's the thin end of the wedge and I may eventually lose my job
- my special skills are no longer required
- I will have less freedom
- I may lose some of my friends and personal contacts
- I will have less responsibility
- it will cause more problems than it's worth
- it's only one year since they made the last change
- I resent being told what to do
- they never asked me for my ideas
- I built up the present system and now they say it's not good enough
- I will lose my status and authority
- it will bring extra work

*Facilitating Change*

- I don't think I have the necessary skills
- I've been kept in the dark
- I believe the change doesn't make sense for our organization
- I don't think that the initiators understand everything they need to.

People's perceptions and attitudes are based on the way in which they are invited to contribute and how they feel they are treated before, during and after the change. Comments such as those listed here would provoke in me a desire, a need to enquire further, a wish fully to understand the reasoning behind them. I would want to know *why* someone believes a change doesn't make sense for the organization; *what* someone understands by being kept in the picture; *what* someone's ideas are on the subject; *why* someone distrusts the initiators; *why* someone believes we must move forward. This curiosity comes from a number of sources: a genuine interest in people's views; the prospect of learning something new or acquiring some new data; the possibility of tapping into a new line of thinking.

There are some important messages here for those people, like you, who desire change, initiate it and expect cooperation from others. Before planning, or even contemplating any change, you would be well advised to determine people's perceptions and particularly to have an idea of which people might welcome or resist the change and why. Beware of making assumptions about other people's thoughts, feelings and perceptions. Set out to discover these first hand. Chapter 3 of this manual contains a number of techniques to help you achieve this end, including skilful questioning, the use of commentary and effective listening.

## First-order and second-order change

Consider nine dots set out as follows:

• • •

• • •

• • •

Now join the nine dots with four straight lines and without removing pen from paper. Your approach to the puzzle gives some useful clues about the way in which people address change. Many will work for a solution which lies within the box or square bounded by the dots (see solution on page 6). This equates to first-order change, which preserves an existing order by treating any disturbance as something requiring minor adjustment or blocking out. Any resulting change is therefore incremental, tinkering at the edges but essentially leading to more of the same. A characteristic stance would be, 'What are the disturbances and what do we need to adjust?' Typical examples are altering the layout of an office; setting up some skills training to correct a production fault; designing a checklist to ensure that certain tasks are completed; redesigning a report form; changing the composition of a team. An onlooker would see these as cosmetic changes or 'staying in the box' with the wider systems remaining the same.

Second-order change, on the other hand, involves a move away from the constraints of the 'box' (see solution on page 6). Disturbances are treated as information about internal conditions to which the system could respond by altering orders. Such change produces a logically different order from that which came before. Questions which might be asked include:

- Do we really need this office?
- Are we going to continue with these production methods in the longer term?
- How essential are these tasks and do they need to be completed?
- Do we need this report form?
- Is a team approach the best for this situation?

and more fundamentally:

- What is our current situation?
- Where are we going?
- What are the necessary steps to get there?
- How do our values and beliefs match up with our new journey?

Responses could lead to change, for example in corporate strategy, organization structure, job design and management attitudes. Encouraging people to reflect on what has happened in their lives can reveal examples of both first-order and second-order changes. Conclusions can be drawn about attitudes to the different types of change, and with this increased awareness people are better able to understand their previous behaviours and the options open to them in the future.

*Facilitating Change*

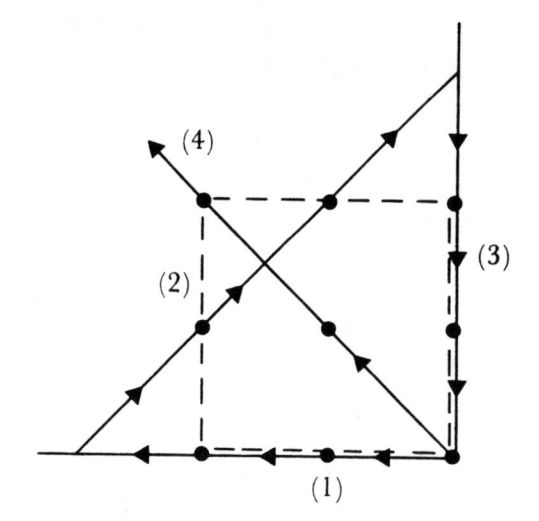

**Solution to nine dots puzzle. First-order change is represented by a broken line, second-order change by a continuous line.**

## Learning and change

For years there was an unchallenged assumption that training worked better for some people than others, often ignoring their preferences or their attitudes to learning; and in fact hardly using the word learning. A common defence for managers, trainers and others who held this assumption was that 'some people won't listen or pay attention' or even 'they will never learn!' Fortunately, much has been done to move from trainer-centred to learner-centred approaches and the work of Mumford and Honey* on learning styles and preferences has greatly advanced our understanding of learning.

Managers and those who facilitate the learning of others now enjoy golden opportunities to influence and bring about change. These arise from the fact that when people learn something it's usually new and that indicates change. If learners move to the point where they use the new learning and incorporate it into their very being – through behaviours, beliefs, values or attitudes – then they will have changed. In other words, learning and change are inseparable and people cannot learn without changing!

Another delightful fact is that learning, or the state of learning, bestows 'permission' on the learner to experiment or do things differently – at the very least the permission to be trying something new without having to get it right first time, or being competent immediately. There will be a cost arising from these trials and experiments because inevitably some will fail.

---

*P. Honey and A. Mumford: *The Manual of Learning Styles* (1986); *Using your Learning Styles* (1986); *The Opportunist Learner* (1990); *The Manual of Learning Opportunities* (1990).

However, this cost is small in comparison with what Peters* calls the 'dire results of failing to support failure'. Dave Boyer, president of Teleflex, Pennsylvania, stated that the key to the company's success rate was its ability to 'fail forward' – that is, to learn fast from failure so as to make the next and smarter step quickly. Central to this is the inescapable truth that negative responses to mistakes and failure will prevent learning.

Change which is tackled under the umbrella of learning is legitimate, thus removing or reducing many of the obstacles perceived by learners about what others might think, feel, see or say.

## The learning activities

The learning activities in Part II all relate to the core theme of change: they move from the individual, through the team and organization into the environment. The word change has various connotations and within the activities you will recognize many words reflecting this: for example, raise, reduce, increase, heighten, improve, widen, trigger, create, discover and innovate. A starting point is that most change comes from within individuals. People can be equipped with new skills and knowledge, but before they apply these, and thereby change, they need to feel the will and possess the positive attitudes to do so. As someone conducting these activities you will have a prime role to play in creating a supportive climate from which changes can flow.

Because the activities have been designed to stand alone they can be applied to identified needs either singly or in combination. The wise manager will wish to ensure that, however they are used, they form an integral part of a wider process of learning or development. Participants will need to see the relevance of the activities to their own needs and aspirations and will also wish to see how the learning can be applied to their future.

The matrix index at the start of Part II will help you to see connections between the activities and the various themes in this manual. It provides a quick overview of all the activity titles and where the use of video filming could enhance the feedback available to participants.

Where individual use is indicated, the language in the activity is aimed directly at the learner or participant. For group use the language is directed to you as the person conducting the activity. Some group activities include a comment, under the section describing what the activity is designed for, suggesting that they can be adapted for individual use. If you choose to adapt them it is best to incorporate a number of progress review meetings with the individual pursuing the activity.

The activities are applicable in a number of situations: for example during meetings of your team, by individuals after discussion with yourself, by

---

*Tom Peters, Thriving on Chaos, Pan/Macmillan, London, 1988.

individuals on their own initiative or by yourself for your own benefit. All activities follow a standard format:

- brief description
- benefits
- who it is suitable for
- what to do
- time required
- resources and materials needed.

This format will help you to select activities which match identified learning needs and objectives. This is discussed further in Chapter 4.

# Symbol

Document sheet

# Part I
# Helping your staff to learn

# 1
# Management, learning and the management of learning

**A recap on managing**

Much has been written about managing and management and this manual is not the place to repeat earlier work. However, a few minutes spent considering what characterizes successful management will pay dividends in shaping your thinking about the development of yourself and your staff. The bare essentials of a successful management process are shown in Figure 1.1.

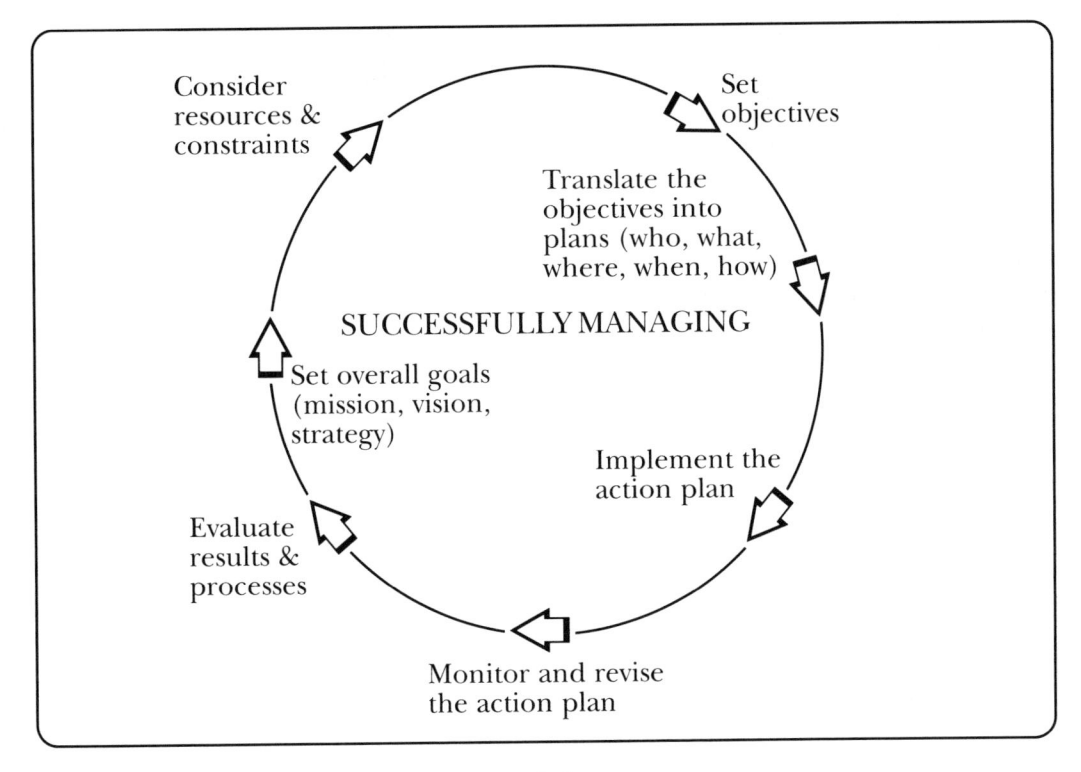

Figure 1.1. A successful management process

The crux of effective management lies in the competence of the people who are engaged in each stage of the process. Take a few minutes to think about your own organization and consider who is involved at each stage. You will probably conclude that you and your staff have a potential impact on most stages, probably more so than first seemed the case. There is a strong connection between skill levels and the effectiveness of the management process as a whole, and therefore it is easy to appreciate the value of investing in the learning and development of yourself and your staff.

Much recent attention has concentrated on defining occupational standards of competence for managers and highlighting the skills, knowledge and abilities they require to perform their role effectively. The standards confirm and reflect the fundamental requirement for managers to be able to work with other people, both inside and outside the organization. Here, for example, are some extracts from the Management Charter Initiative (MCI) Occupational Standards for Managers, sponsored and funded by the National Forum for Management Education and Development and the Department of Employment (UK, 1991):

> While job titles and accountabilities may vary there are many common features in the roles they [managers] undertake. All will be responsible for the direction and control of the activities of other people, achievement of results and the efficient and effective use of the resources provided to them.
>
> As well as dividing up and managing the flow of work, setting performance targets, developing their staff, providing instructions, monitoring and controlling progress against objectives, there is likely to be a good deal of negotiation and discussion with colleagues as well as giving feedback to others.

A closer examination of the occupational standards reveals a clear onus of responsibility placed on managers to 'develop teams, individuals and self to enhance performance'. The constituent parts of this responsibility are described thus:

the competent manager will be involved in:

- self development;
- assessment of current competence of self and staff;
- analysing learning and development needs;
- planning to meet these needs;
- ensuring that appropriate development takes place;
- reviewing progress.

## A recap on learning

In the same way that management can be viewed as a cyclical, continuously developing process, so too can learning. Many people know that learning does not stem from experience alone and this is supported by the concept of a 'learning cycle' (see Figure 1.2).

For learning to occur, all stages of the cycle need attention. It is obvious that some people show a preference for one or two stages of the learning cycle, thus neglecting the others. For example, can you think of people in your organization who spend their time rushing from one problem to the next, never stopping to think and reflect on how to prevent particular problems from recurring? Regrettably, such people may be perceived as being 'in a rut', lacking in imagination and unwilling to change. Are there others who appear preoccupied with analysing what has happened, suggesting new ways of doing things but seldom putting these ideas into practice? These may be labelled by others as 'talkers' rather than 'doers'.

A more positive way of regarding such people is that they may not appreciate the learning process in its entirety. By introducing them to the notion of a learning cycle, and by offering encouragement and support throughout each stage, their capacity to learn can be enhanced. As a manager you are ideally placed to help your staff with each stage of their

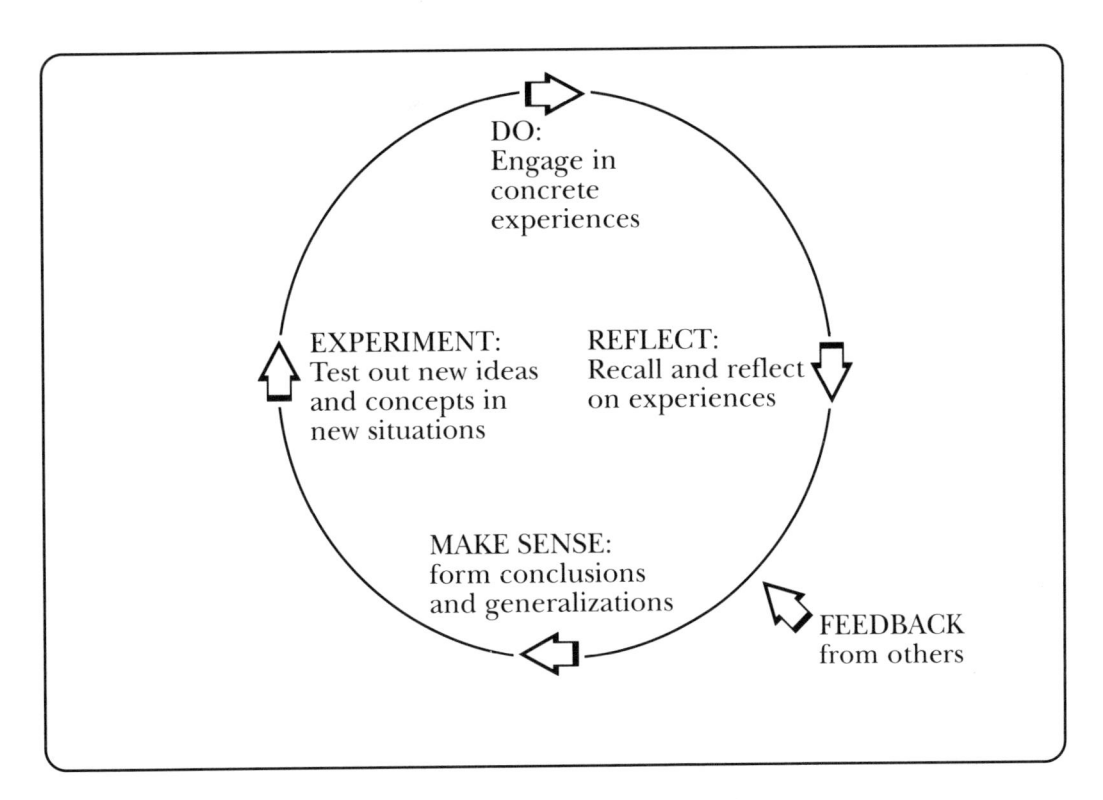

Figure 1.2. A learning cycle
(adapted from Kolb, D., *Experiential Learning* (Prentice Hall, 1984))

learning, and the final section of this chapter includes a number of actions which you can take to do this.

Furthermore, the learning cycle has been incorporated into the design of all activities in Part II of this manual. This means that by following each stage described in an activity the user will automatically be guided through the component parts of a learning cycle, thus raising the potential for learning to take place. You can help in this process by encouraging your staff to complete all stages of an activity, as described under the heading 'What to do', especially any stages which they, or you, may feel tempted to leave out.

## Feedback

You will see that the learning cycle includes feedback from others as an integral part of the process. This is because it is difficult to reflect on and make sense of our actions on our own. Other people have perceptions of our behaviour which place them in a better position to provide us with potentially valuable data to help us to form a clearer picture of ourselves. Giving and receiving feedback do not come naturally to many people, probably because of a lack of appreciation of its value. There are some simple actions we can all take to bring feedback into the learning equation.

When *giving* feedback:

- check that the other person is receptive;
- address the other person directly – face to face, with eye contact, using their name;
- be specific;
- be clear that these are your reactions to the other person's behaviour;
- avoid blaming;
- avoid judging;
- avoid interpreting;
- offer feedback as information, free from attached conditions;
- avoid giving too much feedback at one time.

When *receiving* feedback:

- let others know that their feedback is important to you;
- encourage the sender to provide the feedback – treat it as a gift;
- be prepared to receive feedback as information about yourself;

- decide for yourself what to do with the information – for example, accept it, reject it, wholly or partly, or check it out with others;
- avoid arguing with the sender;
- seek clarification only if you do not understand the feedback;
- avoid justifying those aspects of your behaviour which led to the feedback;
- avoid denying the feedback;
- thank the person for providing the feedback.

## A closer look at learning

At one level there is what is called single-loop learning, a process that involves detecting and correcting errors to permit an organization to carry on its present policies or achieve its present objectives. This is more akin to training – with the notion of putting things right. Staff are taught to get it right, to know the system, to form appropriate habits and to behave in the correct way. This is little more than conditioning, something which is done *to* people, giving them little, if any, room to challenge existing methods and procedures. At best the outcome is conformity to a norm, stifling initiative and creativity.

Double-loop learning on the other hand, is much more liberating, in that it allows a second look at the situation through questioning the relevance of existing norms. This questioning will not automatically lead to a modification of existing goals, methods and procedures, but it does allow for this possibility. Unfortunately some cultures make it impossible to question or enquire into underlying norms, for example because of power distribution. There may be intolerance of challenge and confrontation; it is considered better to say nothing, or to camouflage feelings or appear to comply with espoused policies and practices. And then what? Camouflage or collusion keeps hidden the very information needed for double-loop learning. If people in power cannot be questioned or challenged there is a high price to pay, for they will always be expected to be the all-knowing, learned ones. You are well placed to make a judgement about the type of organizational culture within which you operate. The section in Chapter 2 entitled 'Organizational learning culture' offers you a framework which can be used for this purpose.

## Learning about learning

> Give a person a fish and they eat for a day: enable a person to fish and they eat for a lifetime.

*Facilitating Change*

If people can be helped to learn how to learn they will have acquired a lifelong gift. Not least they will be in touch with the types of situations and processes from which they have learned in the past, thus they will be in a strong position to create the conditions in which they can continue to learn and develop in the future.

John Morris* suggests that organizational members need to recognize that part of their purpose is to manage their own learning, to become aware of how they are currently learning, and to find ways of improving this learning.

## The parts people play

The learning process flourishes when all the parties involved are behaving in appropriate ways.

In ideal circumstances individual learners show interest in their own development, articulate their needs and initiate and drive the process. Their managers, and others, create opportunities, offer encouragement and support their learning. The organization provides a positive climate within which learning can occur and where the pursuit of learning is seen as a legitimate activity.

## Linking managing to learning

Figure 1.3 shows what happens when management and learning are combined.

There are some actions that you can take as a manager to drive and support the learning process, both for yourself and your staff. These actions correspond to the four stages of the learning cycle, and indicate opportunities for providing feedback.

### DO: Engage in concrete experiences

- Show interest in what staff do.
- Be clear with staff about what is expected.
- Help staff to set and understand standards and targets.
- Offer support and encouragement to staff in what they do.
- Create opportunities for staff to do things.

---

*John Morris 'Development work and the learning spiral' in Mumford, A. (ed.), *Gower Handbook of Management Development*, Gower, 1994, fourth edition.

## The management of learning cycle

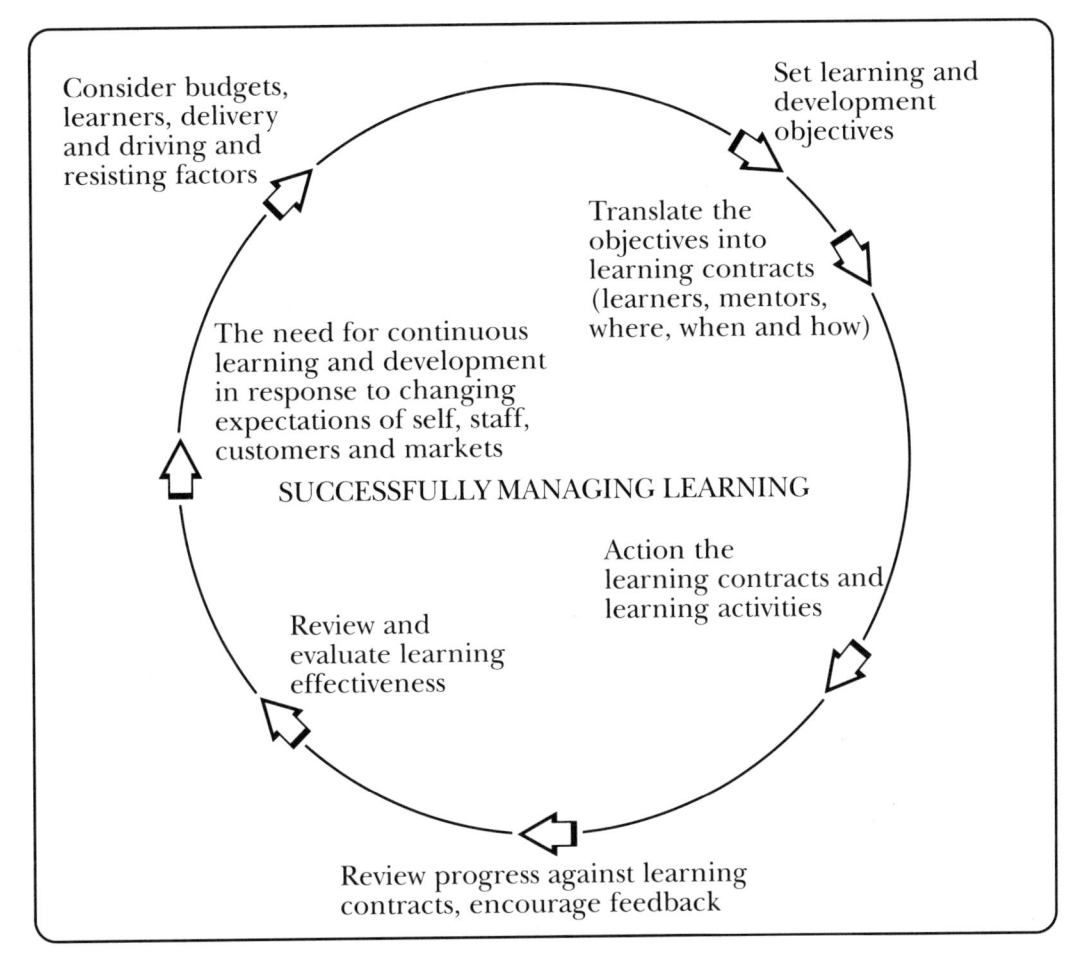

- Set learning and development objectives
- Translate the objectives into learning contracts (learners, mentors, where, when and how)
- Action the learning contracts and learning activities
- Review progress against learning contracts, encourage feedback
- Review and evaluate learning effectiveness
- The need for continuous learning and development in response to changing expectations of self, staff, customers and markets
- Consider budgets, learners, delivery and driving and resisting factors

**SUCCESSFULLY MANAGING LEARNING**

Figure 1.3. The management of learning

## *REFLECT: Recall and reflect on experiences*

- Encourage staff to describe what they have done – seek commentary on their observations, thoughts and feelings.
- Give constructive feedback to staff.
- Encourage staff to write down their thoughts on what they have done, for example by keeping a diary, a daily journal, notes of meetings, etc.
- Seek reports from staff on activities they have undertaken.
- Encourage staff to give themselves feedback on what has been done well or not so well.
- Invite staff to review events, meetings, problems, performance, etc.
- Encourage staff to review and evaluate their learning.

- Invite staff to describe their understanding of their own learning processes.
- Encourage staff to question what they have done and the context within which they have done these things.

## MAKE SENSE: Form conclusions and generalisations

- Enable staff to appreciate what they have done well and not so well.
- Help staff to understand the connection between their actions and the results achieved.
- Encourage staff to comment on skills they have used well.
- Invite staff to say what they would like to do differently, and why.
- Encourage staff to write down conclusions on their experiences, skills, attributes and performance.
- Make opportunities for staff to discuss these conclusions with you.
- Seek ideas from your staff on how they can apply their learning.

## EXPERIMENT: Test out new ideas and concepts in new situations

- Delegate new areas of your work to staff.
- Trust staff with new responsibilities.
- Be prepared to take appropriate risks.
- Be prepared to accept mistakes as opportunities to learn.
- Create opportunities for staff to do new things.
- Encourage creativity, inventiveness and innovation.
- Be open to change and continuous improvement.
- Be open to challenges and questions from your staff.

In the activities in Part II you will find that extensive use is made of the 'Act–Reflect–Conclude–Experiment' cycle. By encouraging your staff to follow all stages in an activity, and by incorporating the actions listed above, you will be increasing the chances that learning will take place.

# 2

# Getting to grips with staff development

A friend of mine* put the following question to a group of managers working in his organization:

> What do we mean by staff development?

Here is a representative sample from the responses:

- fulfilling potential for the benefit of the individual, the organization and the wider world;
- enabling people to release talents which they may be unaware of;
- learning new skills;
- helping people to enjoy dealing with what is required of them;
- giving confidence to look forward into new areas;
- a process of framing aspirations and deciding how to get from A to B;
- generating enthusiasm;
- growth in the current role;
- developing to stand still.

A supplementary question, 'Why should we bother with developing others and ourselves?', produced the following replies:

- to improve efficiency;

---

*Paul O'Mahony, The National Trust, July 1995.

- to be able to perform better;
- so that the organization and the person gain;
- to maintain standards;
- because people are our most important asset: it is only through our people that our other assets and resources come to life;
- to avoid the negative effects of demoralized and unskilled staff;
- to improve the climate of the organization;
- it is fun, interesting and hard work;
- because they want to develop.

We can draw only one conclusion – if we want our organizations to survive and flourish then we must facilitate the continuing development of our people.

## Training and learning

Training aims to change people by doing something to them. Thinking about training usually involves consideration of the inputs necessary to ensure that someone can do something differently in the end. If you are involved in the training of your staff, you will probably be asking the question: 'What needs to be done so that I get the result I want?'

From a training perspective, there is little emphasis on the way in which the individual participates in the process, so the 'trainee' is seen as passive and is expected to respond to the stimulus provided by the manager or trainer.

Learning adopts a different perspective: the concentration is on the learner, their motivation and how they acquire knowledge, understanding and skills. The learning approach involves exploring the starting point from the learner's point of view and then using that information, together with your insight, to plan according to the needs of the learner.

The main point here is that if you take a training perspective, there is a tendency for you to think you know what's best and for you to design inputs for the other person. If your perspective is learning you will wish to start with the other person: you will be interested in what is important to them, how they acquired their knowledge and skills in the past, what helped them to learn and what hindered them, and what they now want to learn and why.

This manual is written from a learning perspective, because I believe it is more realistic to see individuals as active participants and prime movers in their own learning. You are more likely to stimulate their interest and commitment to the process if you start from their point of view.

## Where do you stand on staff development?

- What does development mean to you?
- How important is development?
- What do you see as your part in developing yourself and others?
- Do you think it is someone else's job to develop your staff?
- Do you accept that it is your job and that you have the responsibility to make it happen?
- Do you believe that it is up to staff to develop themselves and that there's not much you can do to influence them?

Your point of view will be a result of your past experience, the experience you have had of managing and being managed, the expectations prevalent in your organization and the extent to which you see your past practice as having been successful.

It may be that you have never considered staff development in any depth – after all, there are personnel and human resource departments who attend to that kind of thing. You may think that it's not your business to do anything about it, especially since there are dozens of other things which crowd in on you and demand your attention. Possibly your own development journey has not been too smooth; maybe no one showed much interest in it.

Perhaps you have a different view, understanding and recognizing the value of developing yourself and others. You may feel a sense of 'developmental expertise': it could be that you're doing it all the time. You may be able to point to your own and others' development successes arising from your personal efforts.

You may feel that the potential benefits to yourself range from many to none; that the costs are affordable to outrageous; that the expertise required is well within your capacity or completely outside it; that staff development is an essential investment or an extravagant luxury. It may be that you don't know where to start or, if you do, you think your efforts will not make any difference. You may question whether your staff will see you as a credible person to be involved in their development.

As a manager you are certainly employed to make a difference to how your company, organization, department or section functions and performs. You are likely to spend a significant amount of your working time with your staff. At the very least you have to keep in touch with them on how their work is progressing.

You could not do your job for long if you did not keep in touch with your staff. Without that contact you would be cut off from vital information and intelligence and would rapidly become ineffective. Unless you know what you can supply to your internal and external customers, you cannot make and keep promises about the quality of service you deliver. And the experience of linking with your staff changes you: it alters your perspective, or, at least, it opens up the possibility that you will not be content with keeping things as they are and that you will want to stimulate change.

Have you ever said to yourself, 'I wish my staff could do that', where 'that' is something like operate the computer program more effectively or get on with their work without constant supervision? It could mean finishing the task more quickly, implementing improvements or getting on better with customers or each other.

It would be surprising if you hadn't had such thoughts. Since you are reading this manual, you may wish that your staff would change their current ways of working. At the heart of your job is a necessity to look for better ways of working. You may want to improve the way in which people cooperate to achieve targets and gain satisfaction from their work.

Managerial work involves constantly searching for better methods of achieving goals and of getting everyone to share a similar understanding of what needs to be done. Inevitably it involves working with and through others to find the best available way and introducing change through influencing people.

Presumably you want to influence people – customers, suppliers, colleagues and your staff – so that they contribute their best to enabling your operation to work well. You may be in a competitive situation, with other companies vying for customers. You may be facing the challenge of reaching or maintaining a set of standards and the consequences of failing to achieve these may be frightening to you. Pressure on you to deliver results may come from others or from your desire to do the best you can, or from a combination of sources. As a manager you are bound to be pressed to get the best from all your staff.

Your perception of your capacity to influence others will make a difference to your conception of your role. If you believe that, no matter what you do, your staff will determine for themselves what they are capable of doing, you are likely to construct your role in a way that remains somewhat detached from staff development. If you believe that your contribution is important, you are more likely to become an active participant in the process of staff development.

How much better it is when you are not the only person searching for new and more effective ways of working! When everyone who contributes to the operation is trying to improve the method of work, the potential for significant and rewarding change is dramatically increased. So it is wise to involve as many of your staff as possible in developing better ways of working.

There is an intimate connection between developing the most effective methods of work and drawing out the potential of your staff. It is by drawing out or bringing forward this potential that you carry out your managerial role to the fullest. No longer is it sufficient for a manager to preside over a stable state; has any really effective manager ever done this? Being a developer of staff is more than ever a requirement for survival.

You could see the effort which you make in developing your staff as a necessary investment in meeting the demands of your job. The goals, objectives or targets which you are expecting to reach cannot be achieved by you alone. You are dependent on the work of your staff, and without their achievements you are unlikely to succeed.

This makes sense, because you need to ensure that your staff have the commitment, understanding and competence to contribute positively, without wasted effort, to the operation for which you have overall responsibility. It is unrealistic to imagine that you can be an effective manager without developing your staff and creating and sustaining the working conditions and culture within which they can apply their potential at work.

## Determining your role

Within your own function or department you can have a direct influence on the 'learning climate'. You can behave in ways which promote learning and development and the questionnaire on page 24 will help you to assess how far you do this. Rank each factor on a scale of 1 (very low) to 10 (very high), according to both how you behave currently and how you think you would like to behave. The completed questionnaire will provide you with a basis for planning the change you desire.

## Understanding the context

People develop through the process of learning. As a manager you can help your staff to realize and apply their potential by creating an environment at work where it is both possible and desirable for people to learn. 'Creating the environment' can mean a variety of things: for example, fostering an interest in growing, developing, expanding and changing, showing why these are important and how they can be achieved.

If staff develop their abilities, there is a benefit to the organization that employs them: the resources that are available for achieving the goals of the organization are increased and the organization becomes gradually more able to do things that were previously inconceivable, impossible or beyond its power. And the potential impact of staff development on bottom-line performance, commitment, quality, innovation and organizational survival is substantial.

Individuals do not develop in a vacuum; they develop within a framework of norms and expectations often referred to as the 'culture' of an organization. The 'way we do things around here' has a huge influence on the way in which individuals frame their own world.

*Facilitating Change*

| I PROMOTE LEARNING AND DEVELOPMENT BECAUSE: | Ranking based on 'actual' | Ranking based on 'desired' |
|---|---|---|
| I encourage my staff to identify their own learning and development needs | | |
| I regularly review the performance and learning needs of my staff | | |
| I encourage my staff to set challenging learning goals for themselves | | |
| I provide feedback to my staff on their performance and the learning they have achieved | | |
| I recognize the important part I can play in developing my staff | | |
| I review my own performance in helping to develop my staff | | |
| I encourage my staff to recognize and seek learning opportunities in the workplace | | |
| I aim to provide new experiences from which my staff can learn | | |
| I facilitate the use of training off the job where learning opportunities cannot be found in the workplace | | |
| I tolerate some mistakes provided that my staff try to learn from them | | |
| I encourage my staff to challenge traditional ways of doing things | | |
| I recognize that most people have the potential to develop their skills and I act on this belief | | |
| I regularly discuss with my staff their aspirations and their potential | | |
| I accept that addressing the learning and development needs of my staff is a priority for me | | |
| I take into account the different learning styles and preferences of my staff | | |
| I offer direct help to my staff with their learning | | |
| I offer coaching, counselling and support to my staff | | |

*Getting to grips with staff development*

# Organizational learning culture

There are a number of features which characterize an organization which supports, and is committed to, the learning and development of its members. You may find it helpful to reflect on these features and draw conclusions about your own organization.

| Feature | Some likely indicators and behaviours |
|---|---|
| Attitude to learning | ○ Seen as the lifeblood of the organization |
| | ○ Top management commitment |
| | ○ High level of interest in members' learning and the application of this learning |
| | ○ Regular and continuing review of members' learning needs |
| | ○ Clear plans are produced to meet identified needs; progress against these plans is regularly reviewed |
| | ○ Recognition of the important role of managers in developing their staff |
| | ○ Encouragement to seek learning opportunities in the workplace |
| | ○ Genuine belief that most people have the potential to develop skills |
| | ○ People provided with, and encouraged to seek, new experiences from which learning can flow |
| | ○ Acceptance that some mistakes will occur |
| | ○ Acknowledgement that different people have different learning styles and preferences – use of a wide variety of learning vehicles and methods |
| Double-loop learning | ○ People encouraged to question the organization's underlying norms, policies and procedures – in some cases leading to modification of these |
| | ○ This questioning welcomed and seen as a key process in the generation of data from which organizational learning can take place |
| Learning about learning | ○ Reflection and enquiry into previous learning methods and experiences |
| | ○ Embedding the results of these deliberations into future learning strategies |
| | ○ High level of understanding of learning processes |
| Attitude to change | ○ Recognized as continuous |
| | ○ Laden with opportunities |
| | ○ Welcomed, not resisted |
| | ○ Inextricably linked with learning |
| | ○ High integration between planned organizational and personal change |
| **Feature** | **Some likely indicators and behaviours** |
| Learning behaviours compared with stated | ○ Behaviours connected with learning are consistent with published policies ('what we do policies is what we say we will do'): inconsistency between the two can be discussed |

*Facilitating Change*

| | |
|---|---|
| Self-direction and self-development | ○ People encouraged to identify their own learning and development needs |
| | ○ People encouraged to set themselves learning goals |
| | ○ People encouraged to seek learning oppor-tunities within their work |
| | ○ Objectives determined via collaborative rather than imposed processes |
| | ○ Members given freedom in deciding means of meeting their objectives |
| Organization and hierarchy | ○ Distribution and devolution of power |
| | ○ Roles, jobs and responsibilities subject to regular change |
| | ○ People encouraged to take decisions on their own initiative |
| | ○ Personal feedback (up, down and across the organization) to aid learning |
| | ○ High levels of openness and sharing, for example, when faced with problems or difficulties |
| | ○ Leaders open minded to the possibility that they may need to change, for example arising from challenges to the basis of their behaviour |
| | ○ Leaders 'supporting' rather than 'telling' |
| | ○ Encouragement of creativity, innovation and the use of initiative |
| | ○ Open expression of differences in, for example, perceptions, values and attitudes |
| | ○ Processes and systems geared to meeting the needs of customers, both internal and external |
| Organizational strategy | ○ Core values, contributed to by all members, clearly understood and widely communicated |
| | ○ Vision, based on accumulated learning of all members, used as a basis for determining future direction |
| | ○ Development of 'resourceful humans' seen as an essential and integral part of organizational strategy |
| | ○ Learning seen as the true competitive edge |

# 3

# Diagnosing needs and recognizing opportunities

**Determining the needs of your staff**

You and your staff can profit from the kind of relationship in which training and development needs can be discussed openly, where the subject is not taboo, where there is acceptance of the possibility that either party can be helpful and supportive to the other. These relationships don't just happen: they have to be built up over time. After all, members of your staff may experience a range of feelings when the subject of their learning needs comes into the open. They may feel awkward or even threatened by the consequences of letting you know about those skills and abilities in which they feel below par. They may not want to disclose what could be construed as weakness.

There is no simple formula for building the necessary trust. However, by showing interest, asking skilful questions and being prepared to listen carefully to the responses you should be able to make good progress. Most people, if they can be helped to feel comfortable and secure, have a wealth of ideas and conclusions about their own effectiveness and a fairly clear picture of the attributes they would like to develop or improve. In preparing to consider the needs of your staff you may find it useful to ask yourself some key questions and to make notes of your responses. For example:

- When did I last spend time with a member of my staff openly discussing their learning needs?

- What examples do I have of giving constructive feedback to members of my staff with the primary purpose of helping them to develop?

- What examples do I have of my staff coming to me and raising the subject of their learning and development?

- How often do I discuss my staff's aspirations with them?

*Facilitating Change*

- What examples can I recall of times when I have created opportunities for my staff to learn something new?

## Indicators of learning and development needs

There are numerous frameworks and concepts which can help in identifying learning needs.

The best learning takes account of those needs which learners recognize for themselves. You can help by encouraging your staff to take stock for themselves; by listening to what they say about their own needs; by helping them to clarify and articulate those aspects of themselves which they are satisfied with and those which they are motivated to develop further. While this is not the only way to become aware of their needs, it should be a significant part of your strategy. Similarly, if you are operating a staff appraisal scheme then you may be able to increase the contribution which your staff make to the appraisal process. If staff are encouraged to self-appraise then they are more likely to own any conclusions, action plans and outcomes which arise from the process.

No doubt there will be some needs which are clear to you. These may result from observations of your own and your staff members' performance, the difficulties people encounter, the mistakes people make. Another set of learning needs come directly from anticipated and/or planned changes. These could be changes in strategy, structure, technology, systems, procedures and so on. You may also be able to identify learning needs arising from current problems or desired improvements.

There are numerous clues and indicators which could point to the need for someone to learn something. Aim for thorough diagnosis and for maximum involvement of your staff in this process. Powerful tools to help you with diagnosis include skilful questioning, use of commentary and active listening.

## Skilful questioning

You will be aware that certain types of questions are more effective than others in obtaining quality information. Many people believe themselves to be skilled when it comes to asking questions. However, if you fail to ask the most effective types of questions, it is all too easy to block, lead or cause a respondent to 'clam up' when the opposite is required. To remind you of the types of questions available, the main ones are listed below together with examples.

*Diagnosing needs and recognizing opportunities*

*Closed*      Likely to lead to a yes or no response. Sometimes this type of question can 'narrow the field' as a lead in to further questions. If used alone it can seriously inhibit the respondent from expressing their views.

- Are you looking forward to this secondment?
- Are you willing to become involved in training and development?
- Did you enjoy the exercise?
- Can you see the value of the proposed changes?

*Open*      Invites qualitative information and free expression of views.

- What thoughts do you have on this problem?
- How could we improve this procedure?
- How can we meet this extra workload?
- Why do you prefer this method?

*Reflective*      Demonstrates that you have been listening. Helps to build trust and show that you are interested.

- Earlier you said ...; why would that be useful to you?
- I heard you say you had ideas for improving ...; what are they?
- You've said you want to develop your skills. Which would you like to tackle first?

*Comparative*      Seeks preferences or clues about the respondent's values.

- What do you see as the main differences between ... and ...?
- How does this compare with ...?
- Why do you prefer ... to ...?
- How does the new method differ from the old?

*Leading*      Presses the respondent towards the answer you desire. Reduces or denies the respondent's choice.

- It's obvious, isn't it?

29

*Facilitating Change*

- Surely you can see the sense in doing this?
- You do understand my reasons, don't you?

*Multiple*  More than one question linked together. Potentially confusing for the respondent and allow part(s) to remain unanswered.

- What do you think about …? Is it … or …? Which do you think is best?
- How do you think we should set about this problem? Who do you think is best qualified and when should we start?

*Forced choice*  Restricts the respondents's options and possibly inhibits creativity.

- Is your priority … or …?
- Shall we engage … or … for this job?
- Shall we stop now or go on for another hour?

*Direct*  Straight to the point. Sometimes can be perceived as insensitive or intimidating.

- Where were you at 10 o'clock this morning?
- Why didn't you tackle it this way?
- What is it you dislike about …?

*Assumptive*  May discourage a response. Could invite argument and damage rapport.

- I suppose that's because they …?
- Isn't that because they can't see the problem?
- Surely they can recognize the value of …?

By carefully choosing the types of questions to ask you will be able to influence the quality of the information obtained. Generally speaking, closed, leading, forced choice and assumptive questions will discourage the respondent and reduce the richness of information available to you. Conversely, open, reflective and comparative questions will enrich the quality of dialogue between you and the respondent.

When you are aiming to achieve high levels of understanding about your staff, there is another dimension to asking questions. Put simply, you can develop the skill of pitching your questions at a particular level; the higher

*Diagnosing needs and recognizing opportunities*

the level the more you are likely to learn about the respondent's motivations. Three levels are described below, together with examples.

*Level 1   Questions to obtain facts*

- What job are you doing now?
- Who was involved in the incident?
- When did you become an assistant manager?
- How long have you worked in the department?
- What training have you received so far?

Sometimes it's important to have the facts; however, facts alone do not tell you much about people. What do facts tell you about a person's interests, ambitions, likes, dislikes, ideas or motivations? You also need to be aware of drawing incorrect assumptions from facts. For example, the fact that someone has worked in the organization for ten years does not necessarily mean that they enjoy it. Nor does the fact that someone has never mentioned training or learning mean that they have no ambition or interest in developing.

Pitching your questions at deeper levels will help you to understand so much more about your staff.

*Level 2   Questions which unlock information on people's interests, thoughts and feelings*

- How do you feel about …?
- What interests you in …?
- How do you think we could go about …?
- What thoughts do you have on …?
- What are the likely consequences of …?
- What would it mean to you if …?
- What would you like to get out of this change?
- What skills would you like to develop over the next year?
- How can I assist you with your development?

*Level 3   Questions to ascertain people's attitudes, beliefs, values and inner motivations*

- Why do you want to achieve …?

*Facilitating Change*

- What is the value of ... to you?
- Why is ... important to you?
- Why do you believe ...?
- What concerns you about my suggestions?
- What are your ambitions for the next two to three years?

A final point on the subject of questioning. You will have worked hard to ask the right types of questions and to pitch these at levels appropriate to the information you are seeking. To avoid undoing this good work, you will also need to concentrate and listen carefully to the answers.

## The use of commentary

If you can understand more about the learner's world you will be better placed to help them identify their needs. Encouraging a member of your staff to talk you through something they have done, are doing or are planning to do – encouraging them to describe their actions, thoughts and feeling at the time – is a source of valuable data. The richness of data obtained in this way will be increased if you are able to listen well and if you can avoid any temptation to judge or interrupt.

Here are some examples of how you can use this technique to increase your understanding of your staff and thereby identify learning and development needs:

*For actions*    Talk me through what you did at the last team meeting.
Tell me what you did when the problem occurred.
Describe to me what you did well yesterday.
Talk me through the things you would like to be able to do better.

*For thoughts*    Tell me what you were thinking when the problem occurred.
Tell me what went through your mind when we missed the deadline.
Tell me what you think about the new computer system.
Tell me what runs through your mind when I mention targets.
Talk me through what you're thinking about the reorganization.
Describe your plan for the meeting with our client.
Tell me how you think we should tackle this problem.

*For feelings*    Tell me what you felt about the sales director's presentation.
Describe what it felt like to be stuck in that situation.
Tell me how you feel about this new procedure.
Tell me how you feel about last month's figures.

Obviously you can ask skilful questions to obtain the same information; however, commentaries can give you more in certain situations. By seeking commentaries you will help your staff to understand more about themselves. By good listening you will become privy to their world and be better able to decide whether you need to do anything: for example, listen more, give feedback, seek further information. Your questions are more likely to be based on what you have heard and thus more 'to the point', relevant and acceptable to your staff.

Try short commentaries to start with; practise the technique and be prepared to experiment. Take care in choosing when to invite commentary and be prepared to describe why you are doing it and to discuss the benefits.

## The rewards of 'active listening'

Several references have been made to the importance of listening to your staff – for example, when they are answering your questions or providing you with commentary. We all tend to acknowledge the importance of good listening but there is usually scope for improvement. To reduce this problem, think about 'active listening' where you convey to the speaker the fact that good quality listening is taking place. You will reap good rewards from adopting the following behaviours when listening to others:

- Decide that you are going to listen from start to finish.
- Maintain eye contact, without staring.
- Put you own agenda to one side and concentrate on the speaker's agenda.
- Demonstrate your involvement by leaning towards the speaker.
- Show warmth and acceptance with nods of the head and confirmatory sounds.
- Seek clarification if you haven't understood something.
- Resist thinking about your next contribution while the other person is speaking.
- Avoid making assumptions about what is going to be said next.
- Avoid finishing the other person's sentences.
- Be honest if you lose concentration for a moment.
- Avoid interrupting.
- Give back what you have heard: paraphrase and summarize.
- Avoid reacting strongly when you disagree with what is being said.

*Facilitating Change*

- Resist interrogation: instead, use encouraging comments and questions such as tell me more; that sounds interesting; what else would you like to say?; what happened next?; how did you feel when that happened?

- Resist the temptation to fill silences (unless you feel that the speaker is uncomfortable).

## Opportunities for learning

Little of what we learn can be attributed to formal training. Our competence in financial, technical, interpersonal, operational and other matters comes primarily from our life experiences. This is not to suggest that learning is an inevitable consequence of experience; in fact, most of us know people whose behaviour suggests that they have learned little, despite the unquestionable variety in their lives.

The workplace itself contains a multitude of possibilities for you and others to learn. For example:

| | |
|---|---|
| attending meetings | being delegated new tasks |
| carrying out special projects | carrying out fact-finding investigations |
| carrying out a cost–benefit analysis | conducting an assignment |
| contributing to meetings | covering someone's job in their absence |
| instructing others | introducing something new |
| leading a team | leading meetings |
| making presentations | networking |
| observing others | observing situations |
| performing the job | preparing reports |
| presenting reports (written and oral) | putting forward a case for change |
| | receiving counselling |
| receiving coaching | shadowing other people |
| selling an idea | taking decisions |
| solving problems | inducting new members into the team |
| taking on new responsibilities | |
| secondments to other departments | |

If you think about how you acquired aspects of your own competence, you may be able to see links between your learning and some of the items in the list. While the workplace offers a wide range of opportunities you cannot assume that doing the things in the list will lead automatically to learning. This is where the learning activities in this manual can prove helpful to you and your staff. They incorporate many of the listed items and have been designed so that the 'doing' or 'experiencing' part of each activity is not isolated. Participants are encouraged to reflect on their actions, draw conclusions and make plans for applying their learning in the future.

## Recognizing what has worked well

Reflecting on what has helped you and your staff to learn in the past can provide some signposts for the future. Remember, though, that people have preferences when it comes to learning; beware of assuming that a learning method which worked for you will automatically work for a member of your staff. With this in mind, you can discover the learning preferences of your staff by asking them good open questions. For example:

- How do you like to learn?
- What has helped you to learn in the past?
- What learning methods appeal to you and why?
- In which situations do you learn best?
- How can I help you with your learning?
- What gets in the way of your learning?
- What things have you found difficult to learn?
- What are the best ways for you to learn?

Should you wish to explore your own or others' learning preferences, the work of Peter Honey and Alan Mumford can be recommended, particularly *The Manual of Learning Styles*, published by Peter Honey, Maidenhead, UK (1986).

# 4

# Confirming the need and contracting the action

Having reflected on your own stance towards learning and staff development, considered the climate within which you are operating and studied the indicators of learning needs, you should now be in a position to move towards some actions. In the early stages be realistic in terms of what is possible, what is acceptable and what is likely to lead to early success. You and your chosen staff must have a high level of confidence that the learning path you are embarking on is likely to lead to some early gains.

If your diagnosis is starting to point towards certain learning or development needs, then check these out with the people concerned to ensure that you are clear about what is required. As with any management process, clarification of what you are aiming to achieve will increase the prospect of achievement. And there is little point in trying to help someone meet a learning need which they have not recognized, nor accepted nor are committed to work on. Energy put into agreeing and clarifying needs is a wise investment.

Familiarize yourself with the learning activities in Part II. These have been designed to help you take action on identified learning needs and the index to activities will help you to arrive at informed choices. You will find that the index gives activity titles and indicates the broad subject areas. Also included in Part II are lists showing whether the activity is designed for individual or group use, together with the time needed for completion. You may like to experiment by working through some of the activities yourself and then answering some or all of the review and evaluation questions given in Chapter 7. This suggestion is in the interests of your own development and to give you some first-hand experience of using the learning activities.

When you have clarified one or more learning needs and identified suitable learning activities, you are ready to agree a learning contract with one or more members of your staff. You need to be realistic at this stage: aim to work on a small number of learning needs to start with, rather than

*Facilitating Change*

several at once, thus reducing the risk of failure. Aim for short time periods which will bring early successes and raise the confidence of yourself and your staff in the approach.

## Contracting the learning

Your chances of meeting identified learning needs will be increased if you use 'learning contracts'. Having helped a member of your staff to identify a learning need you can enter into a formal agreement with them about what they are planning to learn. Several benefits come from entering into such an agreement:

- the learning concentrates on specific, identified needs;
- learning becomes part of a conscious and deliberate process;
- the contract is written and thus more easily publicised and monitored;
- the learning is planned and to a timetable;
- the learner is more likely to be motivated towards achieving the plan.

The focus of the learning contract, that is, what the learner is planning to learn, is a matter of personal choice. The contract is likely to be concerned with skills which the learner wishes to acquire or improve in order to increase job performance. Because individuals will have played a significant part in determining the content of their contracts, they are likely to feel more ownership of the process and a determination to succeed with their plans.

While the format and style of a learning contract can vary to suit individual needs and preferences, the following components should be included:

**Goal** What is the contract about? What might be its title?
For example: coping more effectively with change
raising my capacity to influence others
managing stress
increasing my self-confidence

**Objectives** What skills and/or knowledge do I intend to gain?
For example: achieve cost savings by instigating a change in procedure
increase my understanding of people's resistance to change
identify skills and qualities which I require to influence others
develop my capacity to influence others
identify remedies or options for reducing my stress in the future

|  |  |
|---|---|
|  | increase the number of times when I feel confident |
|  | clarify factors which affect my level of confidence |
|  | identify a number of behaviours to improve my confidence |
|  | identify key factors which motivate me |
| **Actions** | How am I going to achieve my objectives? What do I plan to do? |
| For example: | work through selected learning activities in conjunction with my manager and/or fellow team members and/or work colleagues |

While a list of examples could be given of actions to achieve learning objectives, only learning activities are referred to. These have been specially designed to incorporate all the ingredients for an effective learning process, which means that you, as manager, have a pool of learning materials to draw on immediately. Using the ready-made activities in this manual will relieve you of the need to design and test your own materials, thus freeing valuable time to allow you to concentrate on identifying needs and supporting your staff with their learning.

|  |  |
|---|---|
| **Resources** | What resources will be used? |
| For example: | learning activities |
|  | CCTV |
|  | books |
|  | articles |
|  | support from other people |
| **Outcomes** | What will demonstrate that learning has taken place? |
| For example: | feedback from my manager and fellow team members |
|  | a written summary of two instances where I have influenced others |
|  | a description of three situations in which I have displayed increased confidence |
|  | a short presentation on the benefits of a change I have instigated |
|  | a review of two months' implementation of my plan to reduce stress |

As a manager you can play an important role in helping members of your staff to produce quality learning contracts which stand a high chance of being achieved. They will appreciate your guidance in preventing them from being overambitious. To this end, you may find the use of the acronym SMART helpful. When discussing learning contracts with your staff apply the following SMART test:

| | |
|---|---|
| *Specific* | Is the contract clear and unambiguous, especially in its objectives and planned actions? |

*Facilitating Change*

*Monitored:* Has sufficient thought been given to arrangements for monitoring the learner's progress with the contract? Is it clear who will be involved in monitoring and support and how these will be carried out?

*Agreed:* Have all parts of the contract been agreed between the learner and third parties? Agreements could be reached with yourself, other team members and work colleagues. Through agreement the contract becomes public and more likely to attract support for the learner.

*Realistic:* Are learners being realistic, within their learning contracts, about what can be achieved? Small, achievable steps are a powerful motivator and it is wise to be realistic when setting objectives.

*Timebound:* Is the contract clear regarding the timing of actions, including their completion, monitoring and review sessions?

Attention to the contracting phase of the process will minimize the risk of 'false starts' and increase the likelihood of learning taking place.

# 5

# Using closed-circuit television

Closed-circuit television (CCTV) provides a source of rich material for participants engaged in learning. You may have heard comments such as, 'I hate seeing myself on that screen', or 'I dread the thought of being filmed' or 'I will be self-conscious about the camera'. However, experience shows that once filming starts people quickly forget about the camera. A primary reason for persevering with this technique is its potential to let people see themselves as others see them. Seeing oneself on screen can have far more impact than receiving feedback from others about certain aspects of behaviour.

## Advantages of CCTV

- It is an effective aid to learning.
- The benefit of the 'aha' factor: 'I can now see the effect my behaviour may have on others.'
- 'It's better than I thought. I feel reassured.'
- 'I can see what I would like to change.'
- It provides a permanent record.
- It offers a true record of what happened, with not much room for argument.

## Disadvantages of CCTV

- It can be time consuming.

- There is a need to allay participants' fears.
- Occasionally participants may say, 'That confirms my worst fears.'
- Participants can become preoccupied with their non-verbal behaviours, mannerisms, voices and accents. Subsequently they may attempt to 'correct' these, at the expense of more beneficial changes.

## Guidance notes

### Before filming

- Have the equipment around so people are aware of its presence.
- Be prepared to use it early on; avoid waiting until almost the end.
- Familiarize yourself with the equipment and be prepared to let others operate it if they wish.
- Agree with groups and individuals how CCTV is to be used. To help to allay fears, encourage their ideas rather than imposing your own.
- Think carefully about equipment layout, particularly the position of the camera and the monitor.

### Filming

- Film unobtrusively.
- If filming a group, be prepared to concentrate equally on both speakers and listeners.
- Experiment with starting up the camera and leaving it to film unattended.
- Avoid focusing on hand movements and other mannerisms to the exclusion of other behaviours.

### Playback

- Agree before filming how the film is to be used.
- You may need to edit the material, since replaying everything may be time consuming.
- Consider using a few highlights for the main group and looking at the film in more depth in one-to-one sessions with participants.
- Encourage participants to make their own observations.

- In giving feedback, avoid deflating someone's ego just to provide the opportunity to build them up subsequently.

- Use the film to highlight possible areas for improvement, but limit these to three or four.

- Honour any confidentiality which participants may wish to preserve; be prepared to erase the tape if they request it.

- Offer participants the facility to view their material in private. This presents a powerful learning opportunity and you may be able to arrange for them to keep the tape or a copy of it.

You will need to think carefully about CCTV and the ways in which you can use it to enrich the learning process. If you do decide to use it, remember to allow plenty of time to process the material. CCTV can be a powerful aid to learning but it must be handled with sensitivity and care.

# 6

# Collaborating with others

When considering the training and development needs of your staff and yourself, there are several possibilities for collaboration. The most obvious is to work with training and development specialists if such a department or function exists within your organization. These people have a wide range of skills and experience in designing training programmes and helping others to learn. Many trainers wish that managers would take more interest and become actively involved in staff training and development. They will almost certainly be encouraged by the fact that you are showing interest and looking to them for guidance and assistance.

Examples of the type of help you could obtain from training and development departments include:

- information about organizational training and development strategies, plans and associated activities;
- equipment and resources, for example CCTV, overhead projector, flipcharts, materials and training rooms;
- a 'sounding board' to check out learning needs which you have identified;
- help with choosing appropriate training materials from this manual and elsewhere;
- guidance, advice and direct help in designing and presenting training and learning programmes;
- identifying learning opportunities within your own and other departments;
- helpful advice on the development of your own training and facilitation skills together with constructive feedback on your performance;

*Facilitating Change*

- working jointly in delivering training events and using training activities. This provides you with the opportunity to be involved at all levels, from observing the skilled trainer at work to taking full responsibility for a session and being observed by the skilled trainer;

- evaluating the effectiveness of training programmes and identifying further learning requirements.

By working with training specialists you will be helping them to contribute to meeting the needs of their 'internal customers'. In this way they will be able to make stronger connections between their overall training and development strategies and the needs at the 'sharp end' of the business.

As well as the training department you can also seek support from other departments and individuals. Management colleagues can be invited to become involved in your training initiatives, further enhancing your skills and theirs.

# 7
# Review, evaluation and maintaining momentum

The management of learning is no different from other managerial processes, in that review and evaluation are key components. When we have completed something we can easily be tempted to move on to something else; the pressures we face often conspire to drive us on to the next task. With staff development it is especially important to review what has been done and attempt to evaluate it. This discipline will highlight successes and any shortcomings of the learning process. You and your staff will also obtain valuable data that can be used to enrich the design of learning activities in the future.

Strategically you have more to gain from encouraging your staff to conduct their own review and evaluation than if you carry this out yourself. Here are a number of questions, all or some of which you could use, perhaps in a questionnaire to be completed by your staff following their involvement in learning activities.

## Review and evaluation questionnaire

- What did I set off to learn?
- To what extent has the need been confirmed?
- How far has the identified need been met?
- What do I feel more able to do now than previously?
- Which skills do I now feel more confident with?
- What am I still finding difficult?
- What concrete benefits can I describe as a result of my learning?

*Facilitating Change*

- What has helped my learning?
- What has hindered my learning?
- Who has been helpful to me in taking action on the need?
- What has been their contribution?
- What have I discovered about the ways in which I learn?
- What will I do differently when I plan my next learning contract?
- What further needs have I identified?
- How could these needs be dealt with?
- How can I maintain my learning momentum?
- Who can I discuss these responses with?
- When will I do this?

By encouraging your staff to answer review and evaluation questions, you will be giving them greater understanding of their learning and development. When you discuss their responses you will also become more aware of their self-perceptions, preferences and aspirations, and thus be in a stronger position to continue to support them in their continuing development.

## Maintaining momentum

There is much to be gained from encouraging your staff to take an increasing interest in driving their own development. Your confidence, and theirs, will grow as learning contracts are fulfilled; enthusiasm for learning will rise as people see and feel the benefits of applying new skills.

The learning activities in Part II offer a wide range of development opportunities for you and your staff and you can continue to draw on these as further needs emerge. You may also like to consider the suitability of other learning activities in the Gower series. Together they represent a rich selection of materials to enable you and your staff to take action on identified learning needs.

I would like to think that learning and development will become part of your everyday work, an essential ingredient in your organization's culture and an integral part of the way you do things.

# Part II
# The activities

# Index to activities

The index to the activities in Part II of this book is given on pages 52 to 54.

*Facilitating Change*

# Index to activities

| Activity number | 1 | 2 | 3 | 4 | 5 | 6 | 7 | 8 | 9 | 10 | 11 | 12 |
|---|---|---|---|---|---|---|---|---|---|---|---|---|
| Activity title | Raising my awareness of me | Heightening my awareness of my values | Reordering my personal goals | Increasing my creativity | Raising my confidence | Improving my listening | Overcoming resistance to situations I avoid | Reducing my self-doubts | Letting go of my old behaviours | Widening my support network | Strengthening my motivation | Reducing harmful stress |
| Page number | 59 | 63 | 67 | 79 | 83 | 87 | 91 | 95 | 101 | 111 | 119 | 127 |
| Self-awareness | ● | ● | ● |  | ● | ● | ● | ● | ● | ● | ● | ● |
| Self-development | ● | ● | ● | ● | ● | ● | ● | ● | ● | ● |  | ● |
| Stress and crisis |  | ● | ● |  | ● |  | ● |  |  |  |  | ● |
| Relationships |  | ● | ● | ● |  | ● | ● | ● |  | ● |  | ● |
| Personal transition | ● |  | ● |  | ● |  | ● |  | ● |  | ● | ● |
| Helping others |  |  |  | ● |  |  |  |  | ● |  | ● | ● |
| Communications |  |  |  |  |  | ● |  |  |  | ● |  |  |
| The team |  |  |  | ● |  | ● |  |  | ● | ● | ● |  |
| The organization |  |  |  |  |  |  |  |  |  |  |  |  |
| Equal opportunities |  |  |  |  |  |  |  |  |  |  |  |  |
| Quality and customer care |  |  |  |  |  |  |  |  |  |  |  |  |
| The environment |  |  |  |  |  |  |  |  |  |  |  |  |
| Optional use of CCTV |  |  |  | ● |  | ● |  |  | ● |  |  |  |

# Index to activities

| Category | 13 | 14 | 15 | 16 | 17 | 18 | 19 | 20 | 21 | 22 | 23 | 24 |
|---|---|---|---|---|---|---|---|---|---|---|---|---|
| Optional use of CCTV | | | | ● | | | | | | | | ● |
| The environment | | | | | | | | | | ● | ● | |
| Quality and customer care | | | | | | | | | ● | | ● | ● | ● |
| Equal opportunities | | | | | ● | ● | | | ● | ● | ● | |
| The organization | | | | ● | | | ● | | | ● | ● | ● | ● |
| The team | | | | ● | ● | ● | | | ● | ● | ● | ● | ● |
| Communications | | | | | | ● | | | ● | ● | | ● | ● |
| Helping others | ● | ● | ● | | ● | | | ● | | ● | | ● |
| Personal transition | ● | ● | ● | | | | ● | ● | ● | ● | | |
| Relationships | ● | ● | | ● | | ● | | | ● | ● | ● | ● | ● |
| Stress and crisis | ● | ● | | | | | | | ● | ● | | |
| Self-development | ● | ● | ● | ● | ● | ● | ● | ● | | ● | ● | |
| Self-awareness | ● | ● | ● | ● | ● | | ● | ● | | ● | ● | | |
| Page number | 135 | 141 | 147 | 151 | 157 | 163 | 167 | 175 | 185 | 199 | 215 | 223 |
| Activity title | Making loss a new beginning | Adjusting to the phases of transition | Lessening the pain of change | Raising awareness of the value of people | Discovering ways of helping and influencing others | Triggering my ability to influence others | Discovering new ways to learn | Removing the blinkers | Understanding reactions to change | Identifying strategies for change | Discovering key organizational goals | Developing team goals |
| Activity number | 13 | 14 | 15 | 16 | 17 | 18 | 19 | 20 | 21 | 22 | 23 | 24 |

*Facilitating Change*

# Index to activities

| | | | | | | | | | | | |
|---|---|---|---|---|---|---|---|---|---|---|---|
| Optional use of CCTV | | | ● | | | ● | ● | | | | |
| The environment | ● | | | | ● | ● | ● | | | | |
| Quality and customer care | ● | ● | ● | ● | ● | ● | ● | ● | | | |
| Equal opportunities | ● | | | | | | ● | | | | |
| The organization | ● | ● | ● | ● | ● | ● | ● | ● | | ● | |
| The team | ● | ● | ● | ● | ● | ● | ● | | ● | ● | |
| Communications | ● | ● | ● | ● | ● | ● | ● | | | | |
| Helping others | ● | ● | | ● | | ● | | ● | ● | ● | |
| Personal transition | | | ● | | | | ● | ● | ● | ● | |
| Relationships | ● | ● | ● | | | ● | | | | | |
| Stress and crisis | | | | | | | | | | ● | |
| Self-development | ● | ● | | | ● | ● | ● | ● | ● | ● | |
| Self-awareness | ● | ● | ● | ● | ● | ● | ● | ● | ● | ● | |
| Page number | 231 | 237 | 245 | 253 | 263 | 269 | 279 | 287 | 291 | 293 | 297 |
| Activity title | Introducing change at work | Striving for internal quality | Introducing new patterns of work | Creating customer-conscious attitudes | Shifting our attitudes to service | Improving customer care | Increasing customer markets | Empowering others | Providing a challenge | Taking a risk | Welcoming the unknown |
| Activity number | 25 | 26 | 27 | 28 | 29 | 30 | 31 | 32 | 33 | 34 | 35 |

# Time checklist

This checklist indicates the approximate time required for each activity. For group activities the length of time will be affected by the number of participants.

## Between one and two hours

| | |
|---|---|
| 1 | Raising my awareness of me |
| 4 | Increasing my creativity (without presentations) |
| 10 | Widening my support network |
| 12 | Reducing harmful stress |
| 15 | Lessening the pain of change |
| 16 | Raising awareness of the value of people |
| 22 | Identifying strategies for change |
| 35 | Welcoming the unknown |

## Between two and three hours

| | |
|---|---|
| 5 | Raising my confidence |
| 6 | Improving my listening |
| 7 | Overcoming resistance to situations I avoid |
| 8 | Reducing my self-doubts |
| 11 | Strengthening my motivation |
| 13 | Making loss a new beginning |
| 14 | Adjusting to the phases of transition |
| 17 | Discovering ways of helping and influencing others |
| 18 | Triggering my ability to influence others |
| 19 | Discovering new ways to learn |

*Facilitating Change*

| 20 | Removing the blinkers |
| 21 | Understanding reactions to change |
| 23 | Discovering key organizational goals |
| 24 | Developing team goals |
| 25 | Introducing change at work |
| 28 | Creating customer-conscious attitudes |

## Over three hours

| 2 | Heightening my awareness of my values |
| 3 | Reordering my personal goals |
| 4 | Increasing my creativity (with presentations) |
| 30 | Improving customer care |
| 34 | Taking a risk |

## Between one half and one full day

| 9 | Letting go of my old behaviours |
| 26 | Striving for internal quality |
| 27 | Introducing new patterns of work |
| 29 | Shifting our attitudes to service |
| 31 | Increasing customer markets |

# Individual/group use

## Individual use

| | |
|---|---|
| 1 | Raising my awareness of me |
| 2 | Heightening my awareness of my values |
| 5 | Raising my confidence |
| 7 | Overcoming resistance to situations I avoid |
| 10 | Widening my support network |
| 11 | Strengthening my motivation |
| 32 | Empowering others |
| 33 | Providing a challenge |

## Group use

| | |
|---|---|
| 3* | Reordering my personal goals |
| 4 | Increasing my creativity |
| 6 | Improving my listening |
| 8* | Reducing my self-doubts |
| 9 | Letting go of my old behaviours |
| 12 | Reducing harmful stress |
| 13* | Making loss a new beginning |
| 14* | Adjusting to the phases of transition |
| 15 | Lessening the pain of change |
| 16 | Raising awareness of the value of people |
| 17 | Discovering ways of helping and influencing others |
| 18 | Triggering my ability to influence others |
| 19* | Discovering new ways to learn |
| 20* | Removing the blinkers |
| 21 | Understanding reactions to change |

*Facilitating Change*

| | |
|---|---|
| 22 | Identifying strategies for change |
| 23 | Discovering key organizational goals |
| 24 | Developing team goals |
| 25 | Introducing change at work |
| 26 | Striving for internal quality |
| 27 | Introducing new patterns of work |
| 28 | Creating customer-conscious attitudes |
| 29 | Shifting our attitudes to service |
| 30 | Improving customer care |
| 31 | Increasing customer markets |
| 34* | Taking a risk |
| 35 | Welcoming the unknown |

---

*Easily adapted for individual use.

# 1

# Raising my awareness of me

All too often we can lose sight of ourselves in the day-to-day tasks associated with life and work. We can become trapped in everyday routine with little, if any, time for self-reflection. This activity is designed to help you reaffirm who you are and how you feel about yourself, and to begin exploring what you want for the future. The activity has links with other activities in this manual, particularly Activities 2 and 3.

## Benefits

By undertaking this activity you can expect to:

- reappraise yourself and write a description of how you see yourself in your own words;
- form conclusions about your self-description;
- decide strategies for changing your self-perception, if desired.

## Suitable for

This activity can benefit anyone who is interested in carrying out a personal 'stocktake', for example those involved in personal development activities, the appraisal of life and values or planning a career move.

## What to do

1. Complete the self-appraisal matrix (Document 1.1). This is best done in your own time, free from interruptions.

*Facilitating Change*

2. Discuss your completed matrix with another person, for example your manager, a work colleague or a friend. Invite them to ask questions to help you to clarify your thinking, but explain that you are not seeking criticisms or judgements of your responses.

3. Think about any changes you wish to make and complete an action plan (Document 1.2).

4. Arrange a meeting with your manager to identify the key learning points from the activity. Suggested discussion points include:

- what the exercise meant to you;
- how it clarified your self-perceptions;
- what it means for your future development.

## Time required

1. Completing the self-appraisal matrix takes twenty minutes.
2. Sharing your completed matrix with another person takes thirty minutes.
3. Producing an action plan takes ten to fifteen minutes.
4. Reviewing your learning with your manager takes thirty minutes.

Average total time: one hour and thirty minutes, spread over one week.

## Resources and materials needed

1. Sufficient copies of Documents 1.1 and 1.2 (if required).
2. Enough room to afford a degree of privacy to each participant.

*Document 1.1 (Page 1 of 1)*

# Self-appraisal matrix

|  | **Past** How would I describe myself 3–5 years ago? | **Present** How would I describe myself now? | **Future** How would I like to describe myself? |
|---|---|---|---|
| Who am I? | | | |
| How do I feel about this description of myself? | | | |
| Why do I feel like this? | | | |

Reproduced from *Facilitating Change: Ready-to-use training materials for the manager* by Barry Fletcher, Gower, Aldershot

*Document 1.2 (Page 1 of 1)*

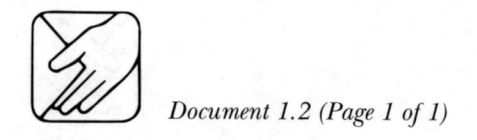

# Action plan

What steps do I need to take in order to change how I feel about myself:

Now?

During the next one to two months?

Two months onwards?

Reproduced from *Facilitating Change: Ready-to-use training materials for the manager*
by Barry Fletcher, Gower, Aldershot

# 2

# Heightening my awareness of my values

Our thoughts, feelings and behaviours often reflect our values and beliefs. Unfortunately the everyday activities associated with work and life can encroach on our time for self-reflection and we run the risk of losing touch with the very things we stand for.

This activity is concerned with increasing your self-knowledge. By reflecting on and discussing your personal values you will be in a stronger position to consider personal change. Participation in this activity can contribute to mutual understanding between team members, thus promoting an atmosphere of openness and trust.

The activity has links with other activities in this manual, particularly Activities 1 and 3.

## Benefits

By undertaking this activity you can expect to:

- clarify some of your key values;
- consider options for personal change.

## Suitable for

This activity can benefit anyone who is interested in carrying out a personal 'stocktake', for example those involved in personal development, the appraisal of life and values, or planning a career move. The activity also has a part to play in team development, particularly for members of a new team or one in which difficulties are being experienced.

## What to do

1. Prepare a statement of some of your values, for example what you believe, hold dear, consider important etc. Your statement may be in the form of words, a descriptive passage, a poem, an illustration or something else of your own choosing. For inspiration you may wish to use Document 2.1, Tuning in to your values.

2. Meet with another person, for example your manager, a colleague or fellow team member, to share your statement with them. Choose someone who is prepared to listen and invite their questions and comments on your statement. Ask for feedback and explore their understanding of your values. They may wish to complete the activity for themselves, in which case you could help to make this happen.

3. Complete Document 2.2, Conclusions from my personal statement of values. Include, as appropriate, any thoughts arising from the meeting at Step 2 above.

4. Meet with your manager to discuss your conclusions and to make a contract about personal change. Concentrate on no more than three areas. One outcome may be: 'I have thought about my values and will not change because …' Any planned changes should be realistic, divided into key stages, time bound and measurable. Agree how you will monitor your own progress and any help and support required from your manager.

## Time required

1. Completing your personal statement of values takes forty-five to sixty minutes.
2. Sharing your statement with another person takes one hour to one hour thirty minutes.
3. Drawing conclusions takes twenty to thirty minutes.
4. Agreeing a contract for personal change takes thirty to forty-five minutes.

Average total time: three hours ten minutes, spread over a period of two to three weeks.

## Resources and materials needed

1. Flipchart paper (if lifeline exercise to be completed), paper and pens.
2. Space to work undisturbed.
3. Sufficient copies of Documents 2.1 and 2.2.

*Document 2.1 (Page 1 of 1)*

# Tuning in to your values

In preparing your personal statement of values you may wish to use one or more of the following techniques:

1. **Lifeline exercise**
   Draw a line on a large sheet of paper to represent your life. The line can be of any shape you choose. Fill in along it important events, achievements, transitions, difficulties and anything of particular significance.

2. **A series of questions**
   For example

   - What was my childhood like?
   - What are the things I still do now which I did as a child?
   - What do I feel about my life now?
   - What is really important to me?
   - What do I like?
   - What do I dislike?
   - What makes my happy?
   - What makes me sad?

3. **Obituary**
   Prepare two versions of your obituary to appear in *The Times:*

   - one which reflects your life to date;
   - one which reflects what you would like to happen.

Reproduced from *Facilitating Change: Ready-to-use training materials for the manager* by Barry Fletcher, Gower, Aldershot

*Document 2.2 (Page 1 of 1)*

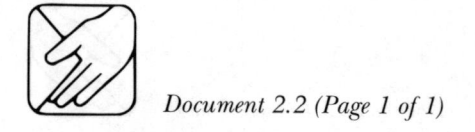

# Conclusions from my personal statement of values

1. What I see as the most significant part of my statement:

2. What I see as possible ambiguities in my statement:

3. How far I think others might describe me in this way:

4. How I think others might describe me differently:

5. Conclusions I draw about myself:

6. Three things I would like to change (include what, how and when):

# 3

# Reordering my personal goals

When we have busy lives we can all too easily lose sight of what we are trying to achieve for ourselves. In quieter moments of reflection we realize that time has passed and we are no further forwards. The fact that our own agenda has been overshadowed by other demands is of little comfort.

This group activity, which can be easily adapted for individual use, is designed to enable participants to concentrate on their personal goals and offers an approach which will increase the likelihood of these being achieved.

## Benefits

Participants undertaking this activity can expect to:

- rediscover the importance of personal goals to their motivation and advancement;
- set personal goals that are meaningful, challenging and achievable;
- work through a systematic approach to produce an action plan for achieving one of their personal goals.

## Suitable for

This activity is for anyone who is interested in identifying goals for personal achievement. Undertaken within a group or team it will help to generate the necessary support between members for personal goal achievement.

*Facilitating Change*

## What to do

While this activity can be conducted on its own, further benefits may arise from doing it in conjunction with Activities 23 and 24 which explore organizational and team goals. Where all three activities are completed, the combined results can be recorded on the T-matrix included as an optional exercise in Activity 23, Document 23.3. Completing the T-matrix shows the relationships between organizational, team and personal (career) goals and therefore the degree of congruence between all three.

This activity also touches on personal values and therefore has links with Activity 2, heightening my awareness of my values.

1. Give a brief introduction and overview of the subject. If Activities 23 and 24 have been completed, briefly review the work already undertaken.

2. Distribute Document 3.1, Reordering my personal goals questionnaire, and ask each participant to spend thirty minutes completing the first *five* questions, either individually or working with a partner.

3. Form small groups and ask each participant to complete Document 3.1, questions 6 to 10, by open discussion. Each group should agree a means of feeding back their findings to the main group.

4. Reassemble all participants and invite each group to feed back its responses to the questions. One person could summarize key points under each question heading using a flipchart, overhead projector or marker board.

5. Issue a copy of Document 3.2, Personal goals, to each participant and briefly explain its use, that is, as an approach to setting personal goals and monitoring progress. The following steps are suggested to help participants complete the document:

    (a) Advise participants that the exercise is personal and should therefore be carried out on their own, in private. However, they may wish to exchange ideas on the application of the document in practice, in which case extra time should be allowed.

    (b) While Document 3.2 is self-explanatory, it may be helpful to work through it using an example such as 'reducing a golf handicap' or 'losing weight' or some other goal supplied by one of the participants.

6. Back in the main group, encourage participants to share with colleagues some of the personal goals they have decided to work on.

7. (optional). If Activities 23, 24 and 3 have been completed, invite participants to:

*Reordering my personal goals*

(a) list personal (job/career) goals in the relevant section of the T-matrix, that is, b1, b2, b3 etc.;

(b) indicate the correlation they think exists between organizational, team and personal career goals using the code indicated on the matrix.

Finally, encourage full discussion on the extent to which personal job/career goals contribute to team goals and, in turn, to organizational goals.

## Time required

1. The introduction takes five to fifteen minutes.
2. Completing Document 3.1, questions 1–5, takes thirty minutes.
3. Completing the remainder of Document 3.1, questions 6–10, takes thirty minutes.
4. Feedback from groups takes thirty minutes.
5. Completion of Document 3.2, personal goals, takes thirty to sixty minutes.
6. Sharing personal goals takes thirty minutes.
7. (optional). T-matrix listing and discussing contributions takes forty-five to sixty minutes.

Average total time: four hours.

## Resources and materials needed

1. Sufficient copies of Documents 3.1 and 3.2.
2. Flipcharts or OHP, paper and pens.
3. Enough rooms/space to work undisturbed.

*Document 3.1 (Page 1 of 3)*

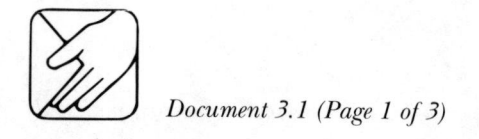

# Reordering my personal goals questionnaire

*Answer questions 1 to 5 either privately or in discussion with a partner*

1. List some of the goals you had at the time of leaving school. They may be serious or ambitious but don't forget the funny ones too!

2. Which goals did you *not* achieve and *why?*

3. What are your goals now?

Reproduced from *Facilitating Change: Ready-to-use training materials for the manager* by Barry Fletcher, Gower, Aldershot

*Document 3.1 (Page 2 of 3)*

4. Why did you change your goals?

5. Suggest ways of prioritising *family, job* (career) and *'self'* goals.

*Answer questions 6 to 10 by discussion in sub-groups*

6. Most people do *not* set down their goals in writing – why is this?

7. Give examples of short-, medium- and long-term goals (consider family, career and 'self' goals).

   Short term          Medium term          Long term

*Document 3.1 (Page 3 of 3)*

8. What should be the main ingredients of clearly defined goals?

9. What, if any, are the links between personal values and personal goals?

10. How might you ensure that some, or all, of your personal *job/career* goals harmonize with the goals of your team?

*Document 3.2 (Page 1 of 5)*

# Personal goals

Most high achievers have an ability to define clearly what they want, when they want it and how they are going to get it. In other words, they set clearly defined goals.

The aim of this form is to help you do just that – to state your goals clearly and concisely and write them down.

Setting goals is the first step, but achieving them involves desire, commitment and a certain amount of patience.

This form will enable you to consider your key goals and to concentrate on one in particular – perhaps one you would like to work on immediately – and to follow a specific routine to achieve it. Once you have worked through the form you may wish to modify or redesign it for your own future use.

## Procedure

In Section A record those goals you would like to achieve in the short, medium and long term. Consider the kind of goals affecting your family and home life (family goals), those which affect your work (job/career goals) and those which are for you alone ('self'-goals). Write your goals concisely in the form of a 'goal statement' and estimate a target date for completion. Finally, decide how often your goal should be reviewed.

*Document 3.2 (Page 2 of 5)*

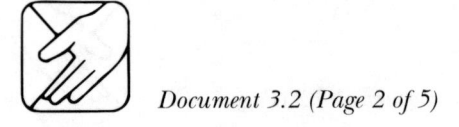

## Section A: Key goal summary

|  | Goal statement | Target date | Review frequency |
|---|---|---|---|
| Short term (under two months) | | | |
| Medium term (two to six months) | | | |
| Long term (over six months) | | | |

*Now complete Section B for one of the above goals, preferably short term, which you are prepared to work on further.*

*Document 3.2 (Page 3 of 5)*

## Section B

1. Write your goal statement simply and clearly including a deadline and quantifying it where possible.

2. Why do you really want to achieve this goal?

3. (a) What is your starting point?

   Strengths (identify those that are critical):

   Weaknesses (identify those that are critical):

   (b) What extra knowledge or skills will you need to acquire to achieve your goal (identify those that are critical)?

Reproduced from *Facilitating Change: Ready-to-use training materials for the manager* by Barry Fletcher, Gower, Aldershot

*Document 3.2 (Page 4 of 5)*

4. What are the main obstacles to your achievement of this goal (rank in order of magnitude)?

5. How often will you review progress?

6. What rewards could you give yourself for success at each stage?

| Reward menu | At review periods (✔) | Upon final achievement (✔) |
|---|---|---|
|  |  |  |

7. What will be your 'measure' of success?

8. Who can you turn to for support in the event of problems?

| Individual/Group | Telephone no. | Address |
|---|---|---|
|  |  |  |

9. Goal action plan:

| List the main steps you will have to take to move towards your goal: |
|---|
|  |

## Tracking success

Most goals can be stated in 'measurable' terms and can therefore be 'tracked' or monitored. It often helps to see this at a glance by graphing results. Time is usually plotted across the horizontal axis and your 'success measure' along the vertical. Typical success measures might be weight (gain/loss), monetary value, score or handicap number, percentage, volume, frequency or time taken.

# 4

# Increasing my creativity

This is an activity, designed for completion during a team meeting or training session, which involves developing creativity when a group needs inspiration, for example when they have reached a stalemate with no immediate prospect of being able to move on. Within the group there may be negative feelings, and difficulties are stated, and blame apportioned with little emerging in the way of new ideas or possible solutions to the blockage.

The activity concentrates on the creativity of each individual and the improvement of group cohesion. It gives participants the opportunity to explore their own and each other's creativity and raises the prospect of these insights being applied in the future.

The result of this activity is that each individual will have prepared a unique presentation, which may include information previously unknown to themselves. Whether or not these presentations are used during the session will depend on the group's own feelings. 'How we got there' and 'how we feel now' are likely to be more important than the product itself.

## Benefits

Participants undertaking this activity can expect to:

- identify the appropriate conditions for creativity;
- experience the enjoyment and satisfaction of doing something unexpected;
- establish trusting relationships which support creativity;
- increase the frequency of group members behaving creatively.

## Suitable for

This activity can be introduced into a team where members feel progress is slow and ideas are not forthcoming. It can also be useful to anyone who is interested in trying something different, exploring their creativity and sharing their ideas with others.

## What to do

Before starting the activity read the following guidance notes:

- This activity should be enjoyable: if it is not then explore some of the difficulties.
- Building up trust is of particular importance.
- It may not be appropriate for every 'unblocking' situation.
- Avoid overemphasis on presentation skills.
- If in doubt, use those parts of the process which 'feel right'.

There is always the risk of allowing people to be too self-indulgent at the 'creativity' stage. You will need to balance this against the risk of cutting off the activity at a vital point, just as progress is being made towards 'unblocking' the problem. There may be more learning as a result of your being prepared to let the creative activity run its course and allow the group to learn about itself and where it goes next.

1. In a plenary session encourage the group to identify and acknowledge some of the difficulties which members believe are blocking progress. Allow fifteen to twenty minutes for discussion using the following triggers if needed:

    - List the difficulties (a 'brainstorm' may be appropriate).
    - Why are we experiencing these?
    - What are your feelings?
    - What might we do to move on?

    Ask the group to draw conclusions from the discussion, including ideas for moving forward. Suggest that one option is to seek new ideas by continuing this activity. If the initial plenary session has unblocked the group you may decide not to continue with the remainder of the activity, in which case it can be kept for another day.

*Increasing my creativity*

2. Distribute Document 4.1, Increasing my creativity. Discuss the document and invite questions to ensure all participants understand what is to be done before starting work. Divide the group into pairs and confirm they have one hour and ten minutes to complete the task.

   You should note the progress which the pairs make without being too intrusive. If you feel it is appropriate you might include a short plenary session of ten to fifteen minutes during this part to review progress.

3. Back in the main group all participants should work together to consider the following issues:

   - What was it like to be creative and what has been learned?
   - How might the learning be used to move on?
   - Is it appropriate to proceed with the individual presentations prepared in Step 2, and if so, how should these be managed?

## Time required

1. Discussion and conclusions about difficulties take thirty minutes.
2. Working in pairs takes one hour and fifteen minutes (including briefing).
3. Discussing the three issues takes fifteen to twenty minutes plus a further fifteen minutes for each presentation (including feedback), if this is the chosen course.

Average total time: two hours, without presentations; three hours and thirty minutes with six presentations.

## Resources and materials needed

1. Sufficient copies of Document 4.1.
2. Sufficient space for groups to work undisturbed.
3. Flipchart, OHP, paper, acetates, pens, tape etc. for people to use with their presentations.
4. Video camera and playback facilities if these will add value to the feedback following the presentations. Participants can view their tapes in their own time, which will not increase the overall time for the activity.

*Document 4.1 (Page 1 of 1)*

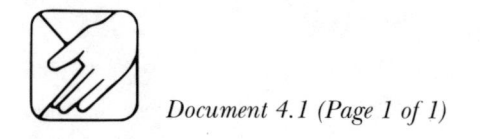

# Increasing my creativity

High levels of trust can be built by working in pairs, allowing each person to express themselves freely. Being provided with good-quality attention from a partner can help to reduce any sense of powerlessness.

After being briefed for this part of the activity, work through the following steps with your partner, aiming to complete all stages within one hour and ten minutes.

1. Spend five minutes each telling your partner about yourself, focusing on something pleasurable, for example an interest or hobby. Aim for 'unconditional listening' in the sense that there are no interruptions or questions during the five minutes.

2. Spend five minutes summarizing feelings about being listened to unconditionally.

3. Take fifteen minutes to help each other decide on a creative way of presenting your selected topic established in Step 1 above. For example, you may wish to use an illustration, a poem, a song, a story, pictures, or give a formal presentation to the group.

   Some key considerations may be:

   - the need to be supportive and yet challenging
   - providing help in clarifying objectives
   - considering various options
   - not seeing a 'perfect' way
   - being yourself
   - agreeing the means of presentation/representation.

4. Take twenty-five minutes to prepare for your presentation. Aim for a presentation which will take approximately ten minutes.

5. Take fifteen minutes to provide each other with feedback arising from the time spent together. You may wish to include:

   - contributions you have received and found helpful from each other
   - behaviours you have found less helpful
   - what you have appreciated/valued in your partner.

Reproduced from *Facilitating Change: Ready-to-use training materials for the manager* by Barry Fletcher, Gower, Aldershot

# 5
# Raising my confidence

All too often, especially when things are not going well, people tend to reduce their self-confidence by dwelling on their own negative attributes and behaviours. If you recognize this trait in yourself then, by progressing through the steps in this activity, you will be able to decide what to do in order to reduce instances where this occurs.

## Benefits

By undertaking this activity you can expect to:

- increase the number of times when you feel confident;
- clarify factors which affect your level of confidence;
- understand how your level of confidence has fluctuated in different situations in the past;
- identify a number of behaviours which could raise your confidence.

## Suitable for

This activity is designed for anyone who has felt lacking in self-confidence in certain situations.

## What to do

1. The purpose of this step is to encourage you to think positively. To start,

*Facilitating Change*

identify those qualities which you possess and which provide you with satisfaction. Typical questions to start you thinking are:

- What do I like about myself?
- What am I good at?
- What are my strengths?
- What have been my successes?
- What qualities do others like in me?
- What do I like to do?
- What situations make me feel good?

Allow yourself to be creative: for example drawing a picture, producing a bubblegram, drawing a brain pattern, or indeed anything which helps to establish your positive attributes.

2. Arrange a meeting with another person, for example your manager, a colleague or a fellow team member, to share your positive qualities. Explain that you would like them to listen carefully to what you have to say and that you would prefer them not to challenge you or form judgements. Invite them to ask you questions and to discuss your positive attributes in order fully to understand your perceptions.

3. Identify *two* situations in the past month when you have felt confident. List the things which you *did* and also the factors which were present in each situation. To help you with this you may like to study the following example:

'Complaining about the poor quality of service carried out by a garage.'

*What I did:*

This may have involved thinking carefully about the dissatisfactions and approaching the garage in an assertive manner with a clear request of what was required to correct the situation.

*What factors were present:*

This is a vital part of the thought process and may involve establishing points such as:

- writing down key points about the complaint;
- getting the telephone number of the garage and finding out the name and job title of the contact;

- arranging to call and meet the contact at a time suitable to me;
- having a 'dry run' with someone I trust;
- visiting the garage, meeting the contact and putting my points clearly;
- checking that my complaint had been listened to and understood and that the contact was clear about what I wanted to happen next;
- gaining clear agreement about corrective action(s).

4. Identify *two* situations in which you have felt lacking in confidence. As with (3) above, list the things you did and the factors which were present.

5. Now make a list of words and phrases which describe *similarities* between your high- and low-confidence situations. Also, list key words and phrases which describe *differences* between the situations. The following example provides an illustration:

One person who completed this activity identified different confidence levels in speaking to groups of people and was helped to list the following significant similarities and differences:

*Similarities*

- Same group size
- Knowledge of subject
- Time to prepare
- Similar room layout
- Similar equipment
- Equal duration

*Differences*

- Venue: for low confidence – unfamiliar; for high confidence – familiar.
- Start: for low confidence – formal introduction from person not really known to self; for high confidence – warm welcome and introduction by person well known to self.

6. Seek the cooperation of another person, for example your manager, a colleague or fellow team member, to help you draw conclusions about significant similarities and differences. In discussion with the other person identify changes which would tip the balance from low to high confidence levels. Transfer these changes into a personal action plan which will include what you propose to do, together with who else will be involved, timings and follow-up arrangements. The following personal action plan was derived from the example in (5) above:

'For the next two months a personal commitment was made to visit venues before making presentations in order to explore and become familiar with surroundings. Also, to meet the introducer for a coffee and chat before the presentation and to agree key points to be included in opening remarks. Agreement was reached to review progress with line manager after one month and two months.'

## Time required

1. Establishing your positive attributes takes twenty to thirty minutes.
2. Sharing your positive qualities with another person takes twenty to thirty minutes.
3. Reflecting on two situations – high confidence – takes twenty to thirty minutes.
4. Reflecting on two situations – low confidence - takes twenty to thirty minutes.
5. Identifying similarities and differences takes thirty minutes.
6. With another person, drawing conclusions and planning take thirty to forty minutes.

Average total time: two hours forty-five minutes, spread over two to three weeks.

## Resources and materials needed

1. Uninterrupted time to complete individual tasks and meet with others.
2. Writing materials and flipchart paper.

# 6

# Improving my listening

The ability to listen effectively is a key skill, one of the main tools through which we can learn to understand others. All too often we listen poorly: our attention wanders; we hear only what we want to hear; we become preoccupied with what we are going to say; we may be listening but our body language suggests otherwise.

This lively group activity involves participants in a range of different listening situations through which some strong feelings are likely to be evoked. The activity is powerful and most participants will learn, or be reminded of, key listening skills.

The activity is appropriate for many situations – standing on its own as a separate activity or introduced in response to recognized obstacles caused by poor listening among members of a work group or team.

## Benefits

Participants undertaking this activity can expect to:

- experience a variety of listening situations;
- discover a range of feelings arising from being listened to in different ways;
- form conclusions about behaviours which enhance listening;
- identify three listening behaviours to practise in the short term and receive feedback on these;
- identify actions to improve their listening skills.

*Facilitating Change*

## Suitable for

This activity can be useful to anyone who is interested in improving their listening skills. It will also benefit teams in their general development.

## What to do

As manager, your role is mainly facilitative: building trust among participants and supporting them through the different 'listening cycles'. As participants take on the role of 'speaker' encourage them to speak about something which they are interested in, for example a sport, a hobby, a favourite pastime, a holiday etc. Some strong feelings may emerge and the benefits of the activity will be increased if participants are encouraged to reflect on these and share them with other group members.

1. Introduce the activity as follows. The exercises within this session are designed to provide some powerful examples about listening. Different listening behaviours will be introduced, with participants being given plenty of time to practise and observe listening and to draw conclusions about the effectiveness of their own listening skills.

    The work will be carried out in small groups of three (or four if numbers do not allow threes) and each member will have an opportunity to (a) listen, (b) be listened to and (c) observe. A predetermined number of cycles will be completed by each group; instructions will be given at the start of each cycle. All small groups meet at the end to share learning.

    Some suggestions for the listening cycles:

    (a) The listener remains passive throughout; no feedback or non-verbal clues to show interest or that the information has been received or understood.

    (b) The listener shows interest and attentiveness, good concentration on the speaker with supportive non-verbal behaviours. The listener refrains from speaking (that is, no verbal feedback or questions).

    (c) The listener constantly interrupts the speaker and is distracted by other events in the room.

    (d) The listener concentrates totally on hearing, receiving and understanding the speaker's words. Questions are asked, feedback given.

    (e) No visual contact *but* every effort is made to hear and understand (as in telephoning). This can be achieved by sitting back to back.

*Improving my listening*

You may wish to design other cycles to suit particular needs or difficulties.

The observer's role is to ensure that the listener keeps to the given parameters and to make notes of any significant factors.

Make sure that all participants understand the three roles and the process in which they are about to take part. Encourage questions.

2. Divide participants into groups of three (or four if necessary, when two observers for each cycle should be used); allocate time and space to each group and commence the first listening cycle. Limit your own involvement to giving clear instructions, time management, organizing the activity and encouraging the groups to record key points at each stage.

At the end of each cycle encourage group members to discuss, offer feedback to each other and record anything which they consider to be relevant to effective listening. In particular, try having them talk about the feelings they experienced when faced by the different types of listener.

Continue until the predetermined number of cycles has been completed, making sure that participants experience each role at least once. Then allow a short ten-minute break before moving on to Step 3.

3. Allow time for each small group to:

   (a) discuss and agree a 'listening model', i.e. those factors which the cycles have alerted them to as being important, for sharing in the main group; and

   (b) help each participant to identify *three* listening behaviours which they are committed to work on, starting now, for at least the next five days.

4. Back in the main group encourage participants to share their 'listening models' and to publicise the listening behaviours to which they are committed in the short term. If practicable, participants can agree to monitor each other's progress and to provide feedback based on observed behaviours.

## Time required

1. Briefing the participants takes ten to fifteen minutes.

2. Each listening cycle (minimum of three cycles) takes twenty minutes (two to three minutes playing the role and the rest for discussion).

3. Producing the model of listening and agreeing each person's new behaviours takes thirty to forty minutes.

*Facilitating Change*

4. Sharing in the main group and agreeing monitoring arrangements takes thirty minutes.

Average total time: two hours forty minutes, which includes a break. (If more than three cycles are completed the time will be extended.)

## Resources and materials needed

1. Sufficient space for small groups to work in (can be achieved in one large room).
2. Pens and flipcharts for producing 'listening models'.
3. Video camera and playback facilities (optional).

# 7
# Overcoming resistance to situations I avoid

Most of us have a tendency to avoid certain situations and, irrespective of the reason for this, we can be left with feelings of dissatisfaction.

This activity, which is most effective when completed with a trusted person who is going through the same process, can help you to examine situations which you consciously or unconsciously avoid. It provides you with the opportunity to consider 'common threads' and to experiment with changes in your behaviour.

## Benefits

By undertaking this activity you can expect to:

- identify situations you would usually avoid;
- identify any behaviour patterns in these situations and reflect on the possibility of change;
- commit yourself to some new behaviours in these situations;
- reduce your tendency to avoid these situations.

## Suitable for

The activity has many applications because avoidance behaviours are within all of us to a greater or lesser extent. The activity is particularly useful when a group or individual appears to be in difficulty, for example:

- where some 'soulsearching' is needed;

*Facilitating Change*

- where there is an undercurrent of hostility and yet confrontation is apparently avoided;
- where there is a lack of openness within a group or between individuals;
- where progress is slow or negligible because of inaction.

## What to do

1. Starting with a blank sheet of paper select about ten situations which you avoid and write them down. Be sure to include some which cause you considerable dissatisfaction as well as others which you feel comfortable about choosing to avoid.

2. Working with someone you feel you can trust, for example your manager, a friend or a colleague, share what you have written down. Ideally the other person will have completed their own list, in which case you can exchange ideas, seeking out common threads and themes in the situations identified. For example, both of you might discover a theme of 'not hurting others' or 'avoiding confrontation or embarrassment'. With a high degree of trust you will be able to question each other, for example:

    - 'Do you feel there is anything missing?'
    - 'What are your feelings about these things you avoid?'
    - 'What are the consequences of avoiding these situations?'

    As a conclusion, for yourself and the other person if they are completing the activity, decide which *three* situations you are most unhappy with.

3. By yourself, reflect on your conclusions and establish areas where you feel some changes might be appropriate. A summary might include:

    - I'm aware of this situation and I feel it's OK to stay the same because …
    - Now I think about it I would be happy to experiment with a change here because …
    - I realize that my avoiding this situation has been counter-productive and I have decided to …

4. Working with the same partner, establish a contract for change. Again, there may be a need to challenge each other by questioning, particularly if there is little indication of commitment to change. For example:

*Overcoming resistance to situations I avoid*

- 'Why not create the opportunity to test that out in the future?'
- 'Thinking back to our earlier conversation, how might you feel if you tried …?'
- 'How might doing nothing compare with making a change?'
- 'What's the worst thing that could happen if you try to change the situation and it doesn't work out?'

In agreeing your contract be specific about the changes you plan to make, the timescale of these changes and how you are going to monitor your progress. You may be able to practise some parts of your plan with your partner, for example by using a short role-play or giving a commentary.

5. Arrange to meet your manager to discuss your experience. Concentrate on what you have learned rather than details of specific situations which you may be unhappy about revealing. Explore the possibility of your manager providing you with support and assistance with the implementation of your plan for change.

## Time required

1. Individually identifying areas you avoid takes twenty to thirty minutes.
2. Sharing with another person and deciding three situations you are most unhappy with takes forty-five to sixty minutes.
3. Individual reflection and summarizing potential areas for change takes twenty to thirty minutes.
4. Working with another person and establishing your contract for change takes thirty to forty-five minutes.
5. The discussion with your manager takes fifteen to thirty minutes.

Average total time: two hours forty minutes, spread over one to two weeks.

## Resources and materials needed

1. Uninterrupted time to reflect and to work with a partner.
2. Writing materials.

# 8

# Reducing my self-doubts

All of us, at some time, question our own value, our competence, our contribution and our worth. These doubts may occur, for example, when we are facing a difficult challenge; when our suggestions have been met with resentment or hostility; when our progress is slow; when we have received harsh criticism or when others have high expectations of us.

This group activity, which can be adapted for use by individuals, examines self-doubts and, while acknowledging that most people are prone to these feelings at some time, enables participants to recognize some potentially positive outcomes.

## Benefits

Participants undertaking this activity can expect to:

- discover the origins and implications of their self-doubts;
- share with others their feelings arising from self-doubts;
- identify behaviours which will reduce their self-doubts.

## Suitable for

This activity can be widely applied, for example:

1. When working with a group which is either inexperienced or lacks confidence in its ability.

*Facilitating Change*

2. To develop further a team where members have established a high level of trust, openness and mutual support.

3. When providing help to one particular person.

4. To answer a 'cry for help'.

## What to do

This activity is likely to be more rewarding if participants are willing to refer to personal situations which involve self-doubt. There may be a need to ensure a climate of mutual support and trust as a preface to the activity and the first few steps are designed specifically with this in mind. You will be assisting greatly by ensuring absolute privacy for participants when they work on their own personal issues during Step 5.

If you are working with an individual member of your staff, omit Steps 1, 2 and 3. Steps 4 to 7 inclusive can be undertaken over a period of two to three weeks with yourself, or another trusted colleague or team member, taking the part of partner.

1. Hold a brainstorming session on self-doubts and ask participants to contribute. Ensure all contributions are recorded on a flipchart using the exact words spoken by participants.

2. Divide participants into small groups and ask them to identify as many causes of self-doubt as possible. Ask them to devise a creative way of presenting their lists within the main group.

3. Bring participants together and agree a process for sharing the results of the small groups and arriving at a consolidated view.

4. Distribute a copy of Document 8.1, Trainer's summary account of self-doubts, to each participant. Divide participants into the same small groups and ask them to read and discuss the account in order to achieve the following aim:

    - Agree and write down a group statement which summarises the *underlying message or moral* contained in the trainer's summary account.

    When each group has written its statement, bring participants together to share and question the statements.

5. Ask participants to form into pairs and reflect on their own instances of self-doubt, followed by mutual sharing of associated thoughts and feelings. Ensure privacy for the pairs and flexibility with time.

6. Back in the main group ask participants to think of positive 'self-talk' statements which can help to alleviate self-doubts. If participants find this difficult you may wish to offer one or two examples of your own or from Document 8.2, Examples of positive 'self-talk' to reduce self-doubts. Encourage participants to write these on a flipchart or whiteboard for all to see. Encourage discussion and questions about the statements. Distribute Document 8.2.

7. Allow time for participants to reflect on the different stages of this activity and to come up with two or three intended behaviours for the future. Encourage the sharing of these in the group and conclude the activity by drawing out people's comments on what they think and feel about the activity and what they believe they have learned about themselves.

## Time required

1. The brainstorming session takes about fifteen minutes.
2. Identifying causes takes fifteen minutes.
3. Consolidating a group view takes twenty minutes.
4. Producing and sharing small group statements takes thirty minutes.
5. Sharing in pairs takes thirty to sixty minutes.
6. Publicising positive 'self-talk' statements takes twenty to thirty minutes.
7. Deciding intended behaviours and the review takes twenty minutes.

Average total time: three hours including a short break.

## Resources and materials needed

1. Sufficient copies of Documents 8.1 and 8.2.
2. Flipcharts, paper and pens.
3. Total privacy for each pair for working undisturbed on personal issues.

*Document 8.1 (Page 1 of 2)*

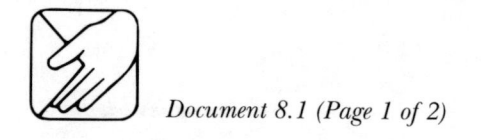

# Trainer's summary account of self-doubts

I recently presented a supervisory development programme in an organization: this involved working with four separate groups over a four-week period. Initially I felt under some pressure and my thoughts were something like this:

- How can I make this interesting to each group?
- How can I maintain interest throughout each day?
- How can I manage groups of such experienced supervisors?
- I am being paid for this so they must learn everything on offer!
- They really must enjoy it!
- If I don't achieve these things I've failed!
- There is no such thing as a bad group!

With my head full of these and similar thoughts, I was experiencing some self-doubt, particularly during the early stages. I found I was coming away from the sessions feeling 'high' one day and 'low' the next.

Eventually, I took some time out to concentrate on what was really going on; by 'tuning in' to my audience I started to hear more clearly some of the things they were saying:

- You look a bit worried: what's up?
- I'm really enjoying this!
- I never would have believed on the first day that I could have done this!
- I found that really helpful!
- I'm glad I made that mistake here; it will be different when I go back to work.

I realized it was impossible for me to carry the burden on my own of expecting over 30 people to react the way I wanted them to. That is, to be fully committed to learning everything they could in an eight-hour day, unwavering attention at all times.

I began to relax and the self-doubts diminished. Concluding that the supervisors were learning, as evidenced by their comments and their doing things differently, I felt I was achieving something. The 'highs' and 'lows'

Reproduced from *Facilitating Change: Ready-to-use training materials for the manager* by Barry Fletcher, Gower, Aldershot

were beginning to even out. As I am writing this I feel like describing a few of my thoughts occurring at this very moment:

- Believe in myself.
- I can handle difficult situations.
- Be genuine: if it's difficult then I'll say so.
- Think of how others feel at the same time.
- Have an objective but don't set myself unrealistic targets.
- Just remember what I can do on the basis of what I've done in the past.

*Document 8.2 (Page 1 of 1)*

# Examples of positive 'self-talk' to reduce self-doubts

- It is natural for me to have some self-doubts.
- If they seem to occur too frequently I should ask myself why.
- I will remember my successes.
- When doubting myself I will recall a difficult situation I handled well and think of the elements which made this a success.
- When faced with a situation which may not work out I know it's worth thinking about those elements which have brought me success in the past.
- It is my aim to make better use of my potential.
- I find it helpful to talk to others about my self-doubts. I like to help others by listening to their doubts.
- I cannot be expected to get everything right, first time, all of the time.
- Some mistakes are inevitable and I can learn from them.
- Dwelling on my self-doubts will hinder the positive contributions I can make.

Reproduced from *Facilitating Change: Ready-to-use training materials for the manager* by Barry Fletcher, Gower, Aldershot

# 9

# Letting go of my old behaviours

This group activity is designed for people who have expressed a wish, together with personal commitment, to increase, reduce or cease particular behaviours. The activity takes participants through a 'checking out' stage in which they explore their desired changes, then a sharing stage in which intentions are announced to others. Next, they have the opportunity to practise the change in behaviour, coupled with support and feedback. Finally, there is some reflection about the learning from the activity together with commitment to future actions, who can assist and how this support will happen in practice.

Following the activity, participants will be better equipped to apply the process to other behaviours which they may wish to change in the future.

## Benefits

Participants undertaking this activity can expect to:

- obtain feedback on aspects of their behaviour;
- decide which behaviours they wish to modify;
- practise some new behaviours and learn from these;
- commit themselves to specific changes in behaviour.

## Suitable for

This activity will be of value to all those who have a receptive attitude towards their own self-development and who are committed to trying to reduce or

*Facilitating Change*

eliminate some of their dysfunctional behaviours. Members of an established team can benefit, especially where there is a recognized degree of openness and trust.

## What to do

As manager, you may wish to enhance your contribution to the process by doing the following:

- Helping participants to understand and apply the skills of seeking and receiving feedback. You may wish to encourage your staff to think about 'feedback contracts' (see Document 9.2). There may be some advantage in filming parts of Step 4, in which case sufficient time should be allocated to view the material. It may or may not be appropriate to view video material in the main session and you will need to clarify this with team members.

- Helping people to define clearly the behaviours they wish to modify.

- Giving good-quality attention and support when new behaviours are being practised.

- Encouraging group members to offer support to each other.

Because of the potential complexity of this activity, a maximum group size of six to eight is recommended.

1. *Preparatory work:* During a team meeting, two or three weeks before the activity is to be completed, distribute Document 9.1, Letting go of my old behaviours: preparatory work, and Document 9.2, Example of a feedback contract. Encourage team members to discuss these documents and to gain full understanding of what is expected as preparation for the activity.

    If people find it difficult to define aspects of behaviour, encourage discussion which should lead to examples such as:

    - interrupting in meetings
    - being silent in meetings
    - seeing the negatives first, rather than the positives, in people's suggestions
    - dismissing other people's suggestions and ideas
    - persistently checking up on staff
    - being defensive when perceiving criticism

*Letting go of my old behaviours*

- giving little support to work colleagues
- listening selectively rather than giving full attention
- aggressive outbursts
- always saying 'yes' to requests
- dominating meetings
- talking too much
- insensitivity to others' problems

Agree a date for the activity itself, which will take up the best part of a day. Allow sufficient time for completing Document 9.1. *The following steps are completed during the day allocated to the activity.*

2. Encourage participants to discuss the progress made with their preparatory work. Ensure everyone has done sufficient preparation to continue with the remainder of the activity.

3. Working in pairs, allow participants time to help each other, through good listening and support, to decide on *one* behaviour to work on. The following pointers may be helpful in briefing participants:

   - choose a behaviour which is easily described;
   - choose something which can be practised during the session;
   - help each other to identify possible benefits of making the change – both to the individual and others – attempt to define these clearly;
   - agree and record a 'contract' which describes what the individual is aiming to achieve, together with ways in which the partner is prepared to assist.

4. Bring participants together and ask them to declare their intentions for new behaviours. If possible, each participant should obtain a commitment from another person to observe and give feedback about progress. The participants now need to practise their new behaviours. Conduct a short decision-making phase to discuss the different ideas and opportunities available to them. For example:

   - group-decision-making exercise
   - role play
   - simulated interview
   - discussion

*Facilitating Change*

- debate
- problem-solving exercise
- short presentation.

One 'vehicle' may suit the needs of one, several or all participants; the main point is to recognize the opportunities for practising new behaviours rather than the 'content' of a particular medium. All delegates must recognize the relevance of at least one of the activities to their own needs.

Allow ample time for completing the chosen items and at the end of each make time for individuals to reflect on and discuss their performance. Encourage feedback which concentrates on the participants' chosen behaviours.

5. Ask participants to return to their same pairs and help each other reflect on the process just completed, with particular emphasis on:

   - feelings associated with practising the new behaviour;
   - what I have learned about myself;
   - degree of enthusiasm for working towards permanent change. If high, then what steps can I take and with what support? If low, then help in defining another area for change

6. Back in the main group, ask participants to discuss their perceptions of the activity, their aims for further change and any opportunities for mutual support in the future.

## Time required

The time taken to run this activity varies because of step 4. However, an estimate has been made based on a group of eight people (maximum) which allows an average of thirty-five minutes for each person for all parts of Step 4.

*Before the activity:*

1. Briefing for preparatory work and giving out Documents 9.1 and 9.2 takes thirty minutes. Completing the preparatory work could take up to half a day per person.

*During the activity:*

2. Introduction and discussing progress with preparation takes ten to fifteen minutes.

*Letting go of my old behaviours*

3. Work in pairs, focusing and contracting takes thirty to forty minutes.
4. Work in main group takes approximately five hours.
5. Work in pairs, reflecting and planning takes thirty minutes.
6. Work in main group and review takes twenty to thirty minutes.

Average total time for activity: one full day (including ample breaks).

## Resources and materials needed

1. Any items or materials necessary for 'vehicles' for practising behaviours under Step 4.
2. Sufficient copies of Documents 9.1 and 9.2.
3. Sufficient space for people to work undisturbed.
4. Paper, pens, flipchart paper.
5. Video camera and playback facilities (optional).

*Document 9.1 (Page 1 of 3)*

# Letting go of my old behaviours: preparatory work

**Stage 1**

Identify three or four people in your organization, department or section with whom you work closely. If you wish, this can be widened to people outside your organization (for example sales staff from suppliers, customers' staff, personal friends etc.).

**Stage 2**

Seek each person's cooperation and describe why you would like them to help. Let them know that at this stage you are gathering data to help with decisions about possible changes in your behaviour. Undertake to listen carefully and explain you will wish to take notes about key points (you may wish to give some people time to respond to you in writing, in which case make sure you clearly agree reply dates). You are recommended to read through Document 9.2, Example of a feedback contract, to help you avoid closing down or resisting potentially useful feedback about yourself.

**Stage 3**

(a) If you already have one or more specific behaviours in mind describe these clearly under Stage 4 (a).

(b) Invite each person to describe clearly one or two aspects of your behaviour which they would like to see increased, reduced or stopped and enter these under Stage 4 (a).

**Stage 4**

Your aim is to gather quality information from other people within the areas (a) to (f):

(a) Behaviour(s) being considered:

(b) Specific examples and instances of behaviour(s) to sharpen focus:




(c) Perceived consequences of these behaviours:




(d) Change(s) other people would welcome:




(e) Assistance other people are prepared to give:

*Document 9.1 (Page 3 of 3)*

(f) Likely benefits arising from your behaviour change:

## Stage 5

Thank people for their cooperation. You could suggest that you would like to discuss your progress with them after completing the activity.

*Document 9.2 (Page 1 of 1)*

# Example of a feedback contract

A key stage in this activity is in co-opting other people to furnish you with information about your own behaviours. Sometimes another person's perception will not match your own; however, the information given will add to the quality of data you possess about how you are perceived. By 'contracting' with yourself to behave in certain ways when receiving feedback, you can enhance the quality of this potentially valuable data.

**When seeking and receiving feedback, I will 'contract' with myself to:**

- encourage the sender;
- receive all feedback as potentially useful information;
- decide for myself what to do with the information; for example, to accept or reject it (wholly or in part), check it out with other people, etc.
- avoid arguing with the sender;
- seek clarification *only* if I do not fully understand the feedback;
- avoid justifying those aspects of my behaviour which led to the feedback;
- avoid denying the feedback;
- thank the sender.

Reproduced from *Facilitating Change: Ready-to-use training materials for the manager* by Barry Fletcher, Gower, Aldershot

# 10

# Widening my support network

Paradoxically, most of our energies are channelled outwards in performing tasks, achieving objectives and in supporting others (giving) with little attention being paid to seeking support for ourselves (receiving). This activity has been designed to help you to recognize and acknowledge the types of support you receive and need from others. It will also help you to explore ways in which you can improve your support network.

## Benefits

By undertaking this activity you can expect to:

- identify current and future support needs;
- decide who provides you with support now and who could do so in the future;
- decide what you need to do to improve your support network.

## Suitable for

This activity is suitable for anyone interested in their self-development. It will be of particular interest to people who have recognized a need to widen their network of contacts to achieve greater personal effectiveness. This need may have stemmed from indicators such as feeling isolation and difficulties in coping with certain situations, or a desire to enhance the range of support received from others.

*Facilitating Change*

## What to do

1. Complete Document 10.1, My support network inventory. The key to this is to think carefully about the types of support which are important to you, including future anticipated needs. As an illustration of the value of support networks you may benefit from sharing your conclusions with another person, for example your manager ('supporter'). Examples of types of support, and situations in which you may need support, could include:

   - coping with crises of confidence and self-doubts;
   - being listened to;
   - being challenged;
   - having access to a 'sounding board' for your ideas;
   - sharing work relationship problems;
   - at times of acute loss;
   - when ill;
   - when feeling overstressed;
   - when someone close to you is ill;
   - when needing feedback on your performance;
   - being helped to review your progress;
   - when wishing to celebrate/share success;
   - when needing to confront senior people;
   - assistance in deciding priorities;
   - assistance with determining aims and setting targets;
   - difficulties with your boss (manager);
   - when needing to take tough decisions;
   - when experiencing difficulties with another member of staff;
   - when falling short with your performance targets;
   - when needing to communicate bad news;
   - coping with being stuck;
   - when instigating change.

2. Move on to Document 10.2, My support network – effectiveness. This

step will help you to explore the effectiveness of your support network, highlighting where it is robust and where there are gaps. Again, you may wish to share your conclusions with another person, or seek assistance in performing the task.

3. Finally complete Document 10.3, My support network – action plan, which is designed to take you from conclusions to action. Refrain from being overambitious. Steps 1 and 2 may have been thought-provoking and demonstrated to you a number of opportunities for improvement. Your likelihood of success in making changes will be raised by being realistic with your action plan. You are invited to aim for an achievement within two weeks; success within this short timescale will motivate you to make new plans in the future.

4. You are recommended to share your action plan, your progress and your achievements with your manager or another supporter!

## Time required

1. Completing Documents 10.1 and 10.2 takes thirty minutes.
2. Sharing your conclusions with another person takes up to thirty minutes.
3. Preparing your action plan, Document 10.3, takes fifteen to twenty minutes.
4. Sharing your action plan and reviewing your progress takes thirty to forty minutes.

Average total time: two hours, spread over two to three weeks.

## Resources and materials needed

1. Copies of Documents 10.1, 10.2 and 10.3.
2. Quiet time with other(s) to share conclusions and review progress.

*Document 10.1 (Page 1 of 1)*

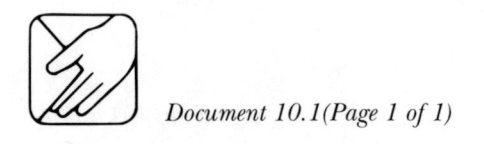

# My support network inventory

| Types of support I need or I think I will need in the future | People who give me support and others who could give me support in the future |
|---|---|
| | |
| | |
| | |
| | |
| | |
| | |
| | |
| | |
| | |

Reproduced from *Facilitating Change: Ready-to-use training materials for the manager* by Barry Fletcher, Gower, Aldershot

*Document 10.2 (Page 1 of 2)*

# My support network – effectiveness

Bearing in mind your responses to Document 10.1, work through the following questions and make notes of your conclusions:

1. Do I have any unmet support needs (currently and for the future)? If so, what are they?

2. Can I give myself support in any of these areas? If so, how?

3. Do I know someone else who could give me support in these areas? If so, who?

4. Have I asked for this support before? If so, what happened?

Reproduced from *Facilitating Change: Ready-to-use training materials for the manager*
by Barry Fletcher, Gower, Aldershot

*Document 10.2 (Page 2 of 2)*

5. What areas of my support network do I need to improve?

6. How can I do this?

7. What help will I need to do this, and from whom?

Reproduced from *Facilitating Change: Ready-to-use training materials for the manager*
by Barry Fletcher, Gower, Aldershot

Document 10.3 (Page 1 of 2)

# My support network – action plan

Working through the following steps will help you to concentrate on those aspects of your support network in which change is desired and also to produce some concrete actions to achieve the change. Sharing the plan with your manager or another existing 'supporter' will increase your likelihood of success in making the change.

1. My support needs that could be better met/and/or my unmet support needs are:

2. For each need, the person who gives me support currently and/or the person who could give me this support is:

3. The ways in which the support I receive could be improved and/or my support needs could be met are:

Reproduced from *Facilitating Change: Ready-to-use training materials for the manager* by Barry Fletcher, Gower, Aldershot

*Document 10.3 (Page 2 of 2)*

4. The length of time this is likely to take is:

5. The area I am going to improve in the next 2 weeks is:

6. The people I plan to review my progress with are:

7. Date(s) for review:

*Reproduced from* Facilitating Change: Ready-to-use training materials for the manager
by Barry Fletcher, Gower, Aldershot

# 11

# Strengthening my motivation

There are times when our personal drive to perform and achieve is lower than we would like it to be. Even routine tasks can seem to be too much trouble and getting started eludes us. This activity is designed to help you reaffirm and strengthen your own motivation and personal drive. By exploring and understanding the factors which have helped you to achieve in the past, you should be more able and determined to achieve in the future.

## Benefits

By undertaking this activity you can expect to:

- identify key factors which have motivated you in the past;
- decide the extent to which these factors motivate you now;
- identify new factors which can recharge your ability to motivate yourself and others.

## Suitable for

This activity is particularly useful for individuals involved in self-development and self-awareness programmes. It can be particularly useful if you are:

- trying to recharge your motivation to enable you to achieve new heights;
- looking for ways of motivating your colleagues and other team members.

*Facilitating Change*

## What to do

1. To get you thinking about the subject you may like to carry out an optional brainstorm on the topic of motivation with your colleagues, your manager or the person introducing you to this activity. For example, try the questions: 'What is motivation?' and 'Why is motivation important?' You could introduce the subject during a team meeting, in which case a number of your colleagues will be able to contribute.

2. Complete Document 11.1, Motivation. If possible, invite one or more colleagues to complete the document and discuss your responses with each other. Make a note of common motivational factors and any other interesting outcomes of your discussions. Arrange to meet your manager to talk through your thinking so far. Use the meeting to address the following questions:

    - Why do we feel motivation is important (for us and others)?
    - What is the activity telling us so far about motivation?

3. Use Document 11.2, Why am I stuck?, to consider something you have been putting off and/or something you want to do but have never got around to attempting. You are recommended to discuss the completed document with a colleague or your manager and to write down what you have learned from it, together with your ideas on actions you could take to make a start.

4. Complete Document 11.3, Strengthening my motivation – action plan, to focus attention on those areas in which you are now prepared to act. Aim to be specific when describing your actions. For example:

    'During the next two weeks I will meet with Jean and Peter to discuss the complaints procedure and to write down our agreed suggestions for improvement. I will request time at the next staff meeting in three weeks' time to present our suggestions and to gain agreement from the full team on changes to be made'.

5. Meet with your manager to discuss your action plan and to agree how and when you will review progress.

## Time required

1. (optional) Brainstorming takes five to ten minutes.
2. Completing Document 11.1, discussing your responses and noting your conclusions takes forty to fifty minutes. Meeting your manager to discuss your thinking so far takes fifteen to twenty minutes.

*Strengthening my motivation*

3. Completing and discussing Document 11.2 and recording your learning and ideas for action takes forty-five minutes.

4. Completing Document 11.3 takes thirty minutes.

5. Discussing your action plan with your manager takes twenty to thirty minutes.

Average total time: two hours and forty-five minutes, spread over a maximum of two weeks.

## Resources and materials needed

1. Sufficient copies of Documents 11.1, 11.2 and 11.3.

2. A quiet room, free from interruptions, to complete documents and hold your discussions.

3. Flipchart, if brainstorming (Step 1) is undertaken.

*Document 11.1 (Page 1 of 1)*

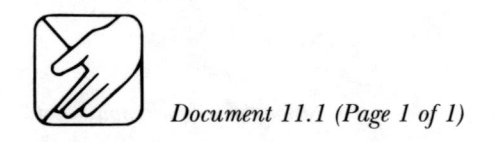

# Motivation

1. How have I been motivated in the past?

2. How am I motivated now?

3. What differences are there?

4. What does this tell me?

Reproduced from *Facilitating Change: Ready-to-use training materials for the manager*
by Barry Fletcher, Gower, Aldershot

# Why am I stuck?

| Situations: | Situation 1: | Situation 2: |
|---|---|---|
| Something I have been putting off, and/or<br><br>Something I have been trying to get around to, and/or<br><br>Something new I want to try. | | |
| *Blockages:*<br><br>What has stopped me in the past from doing this? | | |
| *Feelings:*<br><br>How do I feel about it now? | | |
| *Possible actions:*<br><br>What do I need to do in order to put it into practice? | | |

Reproduced from *Facilitating Change: Ready-to-use training materials for the manager* by Barry Fletcher, Gower, Aldershot

*Document 11.3 (Page 1 of 2)*

# Strengthening my motivation – action plan

1. Which situations from Document 11.2 are within my control?

2. Which situations require cooperation from other people?

3. Who are the people who can help me?

Reproduced from *Facilitating Change: Ready-to-use training materials for the manager* by Barry Fletcher, Gower, Aldershot

4. What do I plan to do within the areas identified:

   (a) During the next two weeks?

   (b) During the next two to six weeks?

   (c) In the longer term?

   (d) How will I review my progress (when and with whom)?

Reproduced from *Facilitating Change: Ready-to-use training materials for the manager* by Barry Fletcher, Gower, Aldershot

# 12

# Reducing harmful stress

*'[Stress is] the state of affairs which exists when the way people attempt to manage problems taxes or exceeds their coping resources.'*
(Alistair Ostell, 'Where stress screening falls short', *Personnel Management*, September 1986)

None of us is immune from stress, whether as a result of work pressures, coping with relationships, bringing up children, facing difficult decisions or any of the many demands which living places upon us. A certain level of stress is desirable to stimulate our interest and our motivation, and it is only when this level is exceeded, as in overstress or distress, that it becomes counter-productive.

This group activity enables participants to analyse incidents which have caused them severe pressure, discomfort or distress. By talking about these uncomfortable experiences with colleagues, new insights are gained through which their 'coping resources' can be increased.

## Benefits

Participants completing this activity can expect to:

- reflect on incidents or situations which have placed them under severe pressure, resulting in discomfort or distress;

- uncover possible reasons or underlying causes which have led to their distress;

- identify remedies or options for reducing excessive stress in the future.

*Facilitating Change*

## Suitable for

This activity will interest anyone who wishes to explore, understand and widen their capacity to manage their level of stress. It can also be used as part of the continuing development of an established team.

## What to do

Much of what has been written on stress is highly subjective and it is difficult to draw clear guidelines from it. This problem is exacerbated by the fact that experiencing some stress seems to be desirable and that 'stressors' – those factors which act on us to produce stress – affect different people in different ways and to varying degrees. At the prospect of delivering a public speech, for example, some individuals feel physically sick – while others will rise to the challenge and enjoy it.

The effects of stress can be grouped into two main categories:

(a) *Mental* – tiredness, irritability, anxiousness, sleeplessness, etc.

(b) *Physical* – indigestion, headaches, palpitations, sweating, etc.

Many stress tests have been produced, including the well-known Holmes Rahe Scale which assigns high scores to traumatic events such as the death of a loved one or divorce, with lesser scores to everyday events such as changes in working hours.

This activity does not set out to evaluate stress in a medical or academic way. Its main purpose is to promote discussion of the subject; to enable participants to share experiences, feelings and views aided by a structured exercise. You can do much to divert participants from the expectation that this activity will provide a 'cure-all'. Instead, the emphasis needs to be on raising awareness and affirming that stress is a perfectly natural state which all people experience.

1. Send each participant a copy of Document 12.1, Stress review sheet, giving sufficient time for it to be completed before the date planned for the session.

2. After a brief introduction, divide participants into two or three groups and give them the following tasks:

*Task A*

Ask each participant to describe their stressful incident recorded on Document 12.1. While each account is being given, other members should listen carefully, encourage the speaker and avoid unhelpful interruptions.

*Task B*

When all participants have finished their accounts, ask each group to discuss the points from these incidents. Distribute Document 12.2, Task B – preparing flipcharts, and ask groups to follow the instructions for preparing two charts.

3. Bring participants together and ask each group's representative to give feedback, using the prepared flipcharts which should be displayed side by side.

4. When all presentations have been made, encourage a general discussion on the issues raised. Useful areas for discussion are:

- the diversity of situations and the different perceptions about what constitutes stress;
- the wide range of coping and stress-reduction methods;
- the spectrum of normal feelings associated with stress;
- the increased understanding and potential learning when individuals are prepared to trust others with their accounts of uncomfortable situations.

Encourage participants to discuss and consider the likelihood that at least one of the stress-reduction methods listed will help in *every* situation.

5. Ask participants to record key points about their learning from the activity and share these in their groups.

## Time required

1. Completing Document 12.1, before the session, should take between fifteen and thirty minutes.
2. Sharing incidents and completing two flipcharts takes forty minutes to one hour.
3. Presenting flipcharts takes twenty to thirty minutes.
4. Discussion takes twenty to thirty minutes.
5. Recording and sharing key learning points takes fifteen to twenty minutes.

Average total time: two hours.

*Facilitating Change*

## Resources and materials needed

1. Sufficient copies of Documents 12.1 and 12.2.
2. Sufficient space for groups to work undisturbed.
3. Flipchart paper and pens.

Document 12.1 (Page 1 of 2)

# Stress review sheet

1. Briefly describe an incident or situation which caused you severe pressure, discomfort or distress.

2. In a few words, describe how you *felt* as a result of this incident. In the box below are some examples of descriptive words to help you.

> fine, grand, lovely, perfect, brilliant, happy, relaxed, calm, confident, angry, subdued, humiliated, funny, peculiar, awful, terrible, tired, weary, exhausted, weak, frightened, scared, petrified, uncomfortable, sick, sweaty, cold, hot, ill, alone, hurt, disgraced, incompetent, silly.

3. On a scale of 0 to 10 record how well you think you 'coped' with this incident.

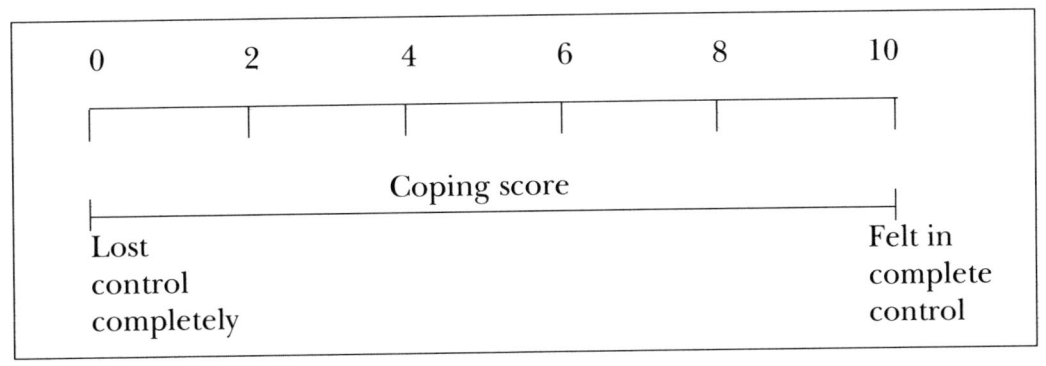

```
   0     2     4     6     8     10
   |-----|-----|-----|-----|-----|
   |         Coping score          |
   Lost                        Felt in
   control                     complete
   completely                  control
```

| 1. Description of incident or situation | 2. I felt … | 3. Coping score |
|---|---|---|
|  |  |  |

Reproduced from *Facilitating Change: Ready-to-use training materials for the manager*
by Barry Fletcher, Gower, Aldershot

*Handout 12.1 (Page 2 of 2)*

4. Finally, describe some methods you could usefully employ to *reduce* or *cope more effectively with* your personal stress.

*Document 12.2 (Page 1 of 1)*

# Task B – preparing flipcharts

Agree who is to take on the responsibility for feeding back your group's findings to the other groups when reassembled. Next produce two flipcharts as follows:

*Chart 1*

| Example of incidents (1) | How did you feel? (2) | Coping score (3) | Stress reduction method number (4) |
|---|---|---|---|
|  |  |  |  |

(a) List all, or a good number, of the incidents reported by participants in column 1.

(b) Record each individual's descriptive 'feeling' words in column 2.

(c) Record each individual's coping score in column 3.

*Chart 2*

Make a numbered list of all the stress reduction and coping methods identified by members of your group when they completed Document 12.1, Section 4.

Finally, complete column 4 of Chart 1 by taking each incident in turn and discussing which of the coping methods might be employed for that situation should it occur again. The appropriate method numbers from Chart 2 are entered in column 4.

Reproduced from *Facilitating Change: Ready-to-use training materials for the manager* by Barry Fletcher, Gower, Aldershot

# 13

# Making loss a new beginning

We all experience loss at various points in our lives: bereavement, redundancy, children leaving home, the end of a relationship, losing our health and moving house are typical examples. Many of us perceive loss as negative. Some people are creative at suppressing the thoughts and feelings surrounding loss and this avoidance strategy can become self-perpetuating and restrict personal development.

This activity is designed to bring loss out into the open, to accentuate the natural process of loss. There is an opportunity for participants to examine the spectrum of loss, to reflect on their skills in managing 'endings' and to recognize the inherent opportunities.

## Benefits

Participants undertaking this activity can expect to:

- recognize the natural process of loss;
- explore the spectrum of loss;
- appreciate your own skills in managing loss;
- share a recent or impending loss with someone else and identify the inherent opportunities;
- highlight some new behaviours for managing loss in the future.

## Suitable for

This activity is suitable within a continuing process of team building where

*Facilitating Change*

members have had time to develop a degree of care and sensitivity towards each other. It can be used when preparing for some impending loss; for example, the closure of a factory or department, a forthcoming redundancy programme or a takeover.

The activity can also be used by individuals who have *either* expressed a wish to develop their skills in this area, *or* who may currently be experiencing strong feelings about a recent or impending loss. In each of these cases you are recommended to provide, or make arrangements for, continuing support.

## What to do

You will need to be sensitive to the fact that the process of persuading people to explore and discuss loss in their own lives may trigger deep feelings and emotive behaviour. By creating a supportive atmosphere, the success of the activity will be enhanced.

In preparation for the activity you should consider your own experience of loss and, if possible, do some background reading on loss, bereavement and transition. You may wish to design short inputs or handouts describing the framework of transition (see Document 14.1) and/or bereavement.

During Step 5, the in-depth sharing in pairs, you will need to ensure total privacy for each group. Sensitivity is also required in cases where participants express a desire for extra time.

Where only one individual is working on the activity, your role is to provide high-quality attention and to facilitate the process. Good contracting together with meetings to discuss progress will enhance the process.

1. There are two options for starting the activity:

   *Option A*

   Ask participants to brainstorm the word 'loss'. This will reveal the different perceptions people have and should produce a number of opinions on the subject.

   *Option B*

   Ask participants to spend some personal time producing their own method of 'tuning in' to how they think about the subject of loss. Personal choice can be exercised here and participants may wish to produce charts, diagrams, pictures, lists etc.

2. Divide participants into twos or threes, and ask them to group and classify the different types of loss. A 'loss spectrum' would be one way of doing this: for example, starting with those losses which are perceived as most severe and moving to those which are seen as least severe.

Encourage the groups to be creative at this stage and to illustrate their work with examples.

3. Bring participants together to share and discuss thoughts to move towards a group classification of the 'loss spectrum'. Almost certainly differences of opinion will be expressed and part of the learning comes from encouraging participants to share these differences. Losses perceived as significant to some may be seen as less so to others.

4. Brief participants for an individual task. Ask them to choose *one* recent personal loss which they are prepared to be open about with one or two other participants. Ask them to write a *brief* description of this loss which they can use in group work during Step 5.

5. Divide participants into pairs (including one trio if numbers dictate this). Try as far as possible to ensure that there is a reasonable level of compatibility between the members of each pair or trio. Confirm the confidentiality of what is to happen next and allocate each group a private area where it can work undisturbed. Distribute Document 13.1 and ask participants to proceed.

    Experience shows that participants involved in this part of the activity may want to continue beyond the time allowed. A flexible, understanding approach is required. One solution might be to include a lengthy break at the end of this stage – those requiring extra time can work on into the break.

6. Bring participants together for a discussion and preserve confidentiality by avoiding discussion of the *specific* content shared within groups. Productive areas on which to focus the discussion and encourage sharing are as follows:

    - the range of feelings associated with loss;
    - the techniques for managing and coping;
    - the important part played by other people during loss;
    - the potential gains arising from loss (usually not recognized until well after the event);
    - the learning, growth and development opportunities presented by loss.

7. In pairs, allow time for participants to share with each other some of their thoughts and feelings about the activity. Ask them to record their thoughts on how they would like to behave when faced with loss in the future, together with the part which others could play in providing support.

*Facilitating Change*

## Time required

The suggested timing is for a group activity. When used as an individual activity you will need to agree lengths of sessions and overall timescale as the activity progresses.

1. Option A/Option B takes ten minutes.
2. Loss spectrum/sub-groups takes fifteen to twenty minutes.
3. Loss spectrum/main group takes twenty to thirty minutes.
4. Personal loss takes five minutes.
5. Sharing personal loss takes forty-five to sixty minutes.
6. Discussion takes twenty to thirty minutes.
7. Future behaviours and support take ten to fifteen minutes.

Average total time: two hours thirty minutes.

## Resources and materials needed

1. Sufficient copies of Document 13.1.
2. Sufficient space for participants to work in private and without interruption.
3. Paper, pens, flipchart paper.

*Document 13.1 (Page 1 of 1)*

# Sharing personal loss

You will need to be fair in managing the time given so that each person has an opportunity to contribute. Use the time to encourage each person to discuss and share their loss. Offer full, undivided attention and help each other to work through some or all of the following:

- What was my loss?
- When was it?
- How did I feel at the time?
- How did I behave?
- What were the high points and low points?
- What range of feelings did I experience?
- What techniques did I use to manage (or cope)?
- What do I feel today about my loss?
- What do I think now (today) about my loss?
- How typical of me was my way of dealing with the loss?
- Looking back, how well did I manage to let go?
- What did I gain from the experience?
- What did I learn about myself?

Reproduced from *Facilitating Change: Ready-to-use training materials for the manager* by Barry Fletcher, Gower, Aldershot

# 14

# Adjusting to the phases of transition

All of us experience transitions within our lives, something which can be defined as: 'the passage from one place, state or stage to another'. Transitions can be planned (as in moving home, getting married or changing jobs), predictable (as in getting older) or unexpected (as in becoming seriously ill or winning a large sum of money).

This activity enables participants, with the help of others, to consider the phases of transition against a background of personal change(s). As a conclusion, participants are asked to think about options open to them in dealing with future transitions.

## Benefits

Participants undertaking this activity can expect to:

- compare the phases of transition with their personal experiences;
- recognize the positive aspects of transition;
- identify the help which they may need from others during difficult times.

## Suitable for

This activity is useful for groups, teams or individuals who are experiencing difficulty with change: for example, in adapting to restructuring, new technology, new systems or procedures. The activity would also complement a process of team development, especially where team members have an interest in increasing their self-awareness.

*Facilitating Change*

## What to do

The concept of phases of transition is likely to be new to most participants and you will need to provide appropriate input. (Some background reading is recommended, for example *Lifeskills Teaching Programmes No. 1* (1980) and *No. 2* (1982), by Barrie Hopson and Mike Scally, Lifeskills Associates, Leeds; *Psychology for Managers,* edited by Cary Cooper and Peter Makin, The British Psychological Society, 1981, chapter 7, written by Barrie Hopson.) As facilitator, you will need to encourage openness and trust in the process of self-analysis and working in pairs. In the concluding session you will help to draw out learning points which may assist participants with future transitions.

1. Introduce the following *three* forms of change and obtain examples of these from participants.

    (a) *Planned:* Intended change such as deciding on a career, changing jobs, moving house, getting married.

    (b) *Unplanned:* These may be *unwanted* by the individual, such as accident, bereavement, loss of job; or *wanted*, such as unexpected promotion, a substantial bequest, winning a prize etc.

    (c) *Growing awareness:* The gradual realization that your life is changing, for example adolescence, approaching middle age, gaining or losing weight.

2. Discuss and explain to participants the basic theory of transition, that is, that the individual will experience a predictable cycle of reactions and feelings with a number of phases. Distribute Document 14.1 which summarizes the seven phases.

    You can expect some debate on the phases of transition, for example the actual sequence. This confirms the uniqueness of each person's experience and the accompanying feelings. Participants may be unaware that in some cases something prevents them from getting beyond the 'minimization' or 'depression' stage.

3. Ask participants to select a recent or current personal transition and, working individually, write down their feelings. Use the following questions to prompt them:

    *At the start:*
    - What were my feelings?
    - How did I react at the time?
    - What helped and/or got in the way?

    *During:*
    - What were the range of feelings?

- What techniques did I use to cope?

*Now:*
- What are my feelings at this moment?

4. Ask participants to form pairs and exchange ideas and feelings. They should concentrate on active listening and other behaviours which encourage each other to be open.

5. Individually, ask participants to decide whether their transition is current or over. Use the following questions to help them decide:

*Current*

- What do I think will happen?
- What do I really want to happen?
- What can I learn from this?

*Over*

- Did it work out as I wanted?
- If not, why not?
- What have I learned?

6. Ask participants to return to their original pairs and share their responses to Step 5 above.

7. In pairs, ask each participant to explore and write down the individual learning points gained from the exercise so far, together with the behaviours and actions which will help with any future transitions.

8. Hold a discussion with all participants together, concentrating on what has been learned rather than facts revealed in the discussion between pairs. It may be appropriate to explore the range of feelings experienced. The following conclusions may help to end the session on a positive note:

- The opportunity (presented by this activity) to express our feelings can help us over difficult times.
- Knowledge of the seven phases of transition may help us in dealing with future difficulties.
- Substantial problems/calamities can lead to personal growth.
- Other people are an important source of help in difficult times.
- We can also provide support to others.
- The situation may seem calamitous but most of the time we will cope.

## Time required

1. Three forms of change takes fifteen minutes.

*Facilitating Change*

2. Discussion on transition takes thirty minutes.

3.–7. Individual/pairs work takes one hour thirty minutes to two hours.*

8. Concluding discussion takes thirty minutes.

Average total time: three hours.

*Steps 3–7 may release some deep feelings among participants and additional time may be requested to bring this part to a satisfactory conclusion.

## Resources and materials needed

1. Sufficient copies of Document 14.1.
2. Flipchart, paper and pens.
3. Sufficient space and privacy for pairs to work undisturbed.

# Transition

The seven phases of transition can be summarized as follows:

1. *IMMOBILIZATION*

    A sense of being overwhelmed, unable to plan and understand. This may be particularly intense where the transition is apparently negative and totally unexpected, for example bereavement (close relative).

2. *MINIMIZATION*

    A denial that the change exists. This has its positive side in that the situation may be too overwhelming to face head-on and time is thus provided to prepare for subsequent phases.

3. *DEPRESSION*

    This feeling emerges from acknowledgement of the need for change apparently coupled to an initial feeling of powerlessness.

4. *'LETTING GO'*

    This is an acceptance of reality but with the knowledge 'I can survive'.

5. *TESTING*

    In the new situation, different ways of coping are tried, sometimes accompanied by feelings of anger and irritability.

6. *SEARCH FOR MEANING*

    After the energy of the 'Testing' phase this is the search for understanding how and why things are different.

7. *INTERNALIZATION*

    Following on from an understanding of the transition, changes are incorporated in behaviour.

**Reproduced from *Facilitating Change: Ready-to-use training materials for the manager* by Barry Fletcher, Gower, Aldershot**

# 15

# Lessening the pain of change

This activity is designed to help people recognize that some changes in life are inevitable. If these changes and their potential consequences are explored, realistic coping strategies can be developed which can be used if necessary. Fear of the unknown is sometimes where the greatest pain from change lies.

## Benefits

Participants undertaking this activity can expect to:

- identify some predictable events which could change their life;
- explore the best and worst scenarios of one of these events;
- develop coping strategies for managing the situation.

## Suitable for

This activity can be helpful to managers and staff involved in strategic planning and/or faced with significant changes in their working environment, for example redundancy, growth, acquisition, takeover etc. The activity also lends itself to individuals embarking on changes in their lifestyle or involved in assisting/guiding others through a process of change.

## What to do

You will need to stress that you are not asking people to predict the future or develop concrete plans which must be adhered to at all costs. The

*Facilitating Change*

objective is to give participants time and space to explore and air some of their worst fears. It also provides them with the opportunity to explore some alternative options and actions. By bringing out fears and looking at them, we can go some way towards reducing them, thus making them more manageable and less painful.

This activity may release some deep emotions to which you will need to be sensitive in order to help participants to begin to work them through.

1. Conduct a brainstorming session on: 'The changes we can predict'. This list could also be generated by asking participants to work in small groups, then bringing all groups together to collate the information.

2. Ask each participant to select a predictable change that could, or is about to, affect them, for example getting older (reaching a milestone age); death of parent, partner, close relative or friend; retirement.

   Individually, ask each participant to list all the negative aspects of the change – the worst possible scenarios. Then after the allotted time, ask participants to turn the lists over and record all the positive aspects and opportunities of the change.

   (*Note:* you may need to remind participants that every negative has a positive if and when we look for it. Change can and does provide us with opportunities.)

3. Divide participants into pairs and ask each pair to share their lists. Partners are allowed to ask for clarification about each other's list, but should not ask their partner to justify or rationalize why they have included something. This particularly applies to the list of negatives. Partners may also challenge their partner where appropriate to encourage and enhance their thinking, especially if they are unclear about the positive aspects of their chosen change.

4. In pairs, ask each partner to help the other to explore:

   (a) Which aspects of the change they feel they have control over?

   (b) How and when they are going to take charge?

   Record responses on Document 15.1.

5. Bring participants together and review the activity and key learning points.

## Time required

1. Brainstorming takes ten to fifteen minutes.

2. Individual scenarios take ten to fifteen minutes to make each list – a total of twenty to thirty minutes.

3. Sharing lists in pairs takes thirty minutes.
4. Completing Document 15.1 takes thirty minutes.
5. Review takes twenty minutes.

Average total time: two hours.

## Resources and materials needed

1. Sufficient copies of Document 15.1.
2. Flipcharts, paper and pens.

*Document 15.1 (Page 1 of 1)*

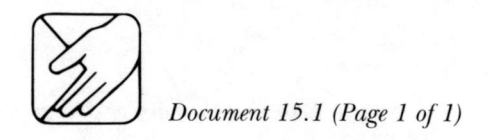

# Taking charge of change in my life

1. Which aspects of the change do I have control over?

2. How can I take charge of these aspects?

3. When will I take charge of these aspects?

Reproduced from *Facilitating Change: Ready-to-use training materials for the manager*
by Barry Fletcher, Gower, Aldershot

# 16

# Raising awareness of the value of people

*'Oh great spirit, keep me from ever judging my brother until I have walked in his moccasins'*

(old Mohican saying)

This group activity explores the differences between people and looks at how to begin to value and make use of those differences.

## Benefits

Participants undertaking this activity can expect to:

- recognize and begin to value differences between people;
- identify the ways in which stereotypes can affect their judgement;
- develop a non-judgemental approach for dealing with people in the future.

## Suitable for

This activity can be used in any situation where it is important for people to be recognized, respected and valued as individuals. For example: in setting up a new team; in bringing new members into an established team; when differences of opinion between team members cannot be resolved; when cooperation between team members is low. The activity will also interest anyone who wishes to explore the effects of stereotyping on their thinking.

*Facilitating Change*

## What to do

This activity can be emotionally charged for both yourself and participants. It is important that you feel able to work with and process high levels of emotions. You need to have a clear understanding of your own values, views and opinions on the issues to be discussed. You may wish to present the activity with a colleague, for example another manager or trainer, to permit a high level of mutual support.

Before starting, prepare a list of questions or statements designed to raise any specific or relevant learning points. Document 16.1, Sample questions, should give you some inspiration, but ideally you will choose subject areas which link closely with real situations, behaviours or problems affecting your team.

Prepare two cards (approximately 30 cm by 10 cm) which state 'AGREE' and 'DISAGREE'. Depending on the questions asked, you may also need other cards which state the different opinions and points of view likely to be held.

1. Read out a question or statement taken from Document 16.1 or one you have written yourself. Place the cards indicating different points of view on the floor in front of you. Ask participants to stand by the card which most closely reflects their own view, opinion or answer to the question.

    Divide participants who hold the same view into groups and ask them to share and discuss why they hold that view or opinion.

    Bring participants together and give them an opportunity, either individually or collectively, to state their case. The other participants can then decide whether or not they wish to change their own view or opinion based on the comments they have just heard.

    (This step is repeated four or five times, using different questions or statements, or for as long as you and the participants feel it is of value.)

2. Lead a discussion to include:

    - how participants felt about being so open with their views and opinions;
    - how they felt if they held a minority view;
    - how it helped them to understand about value and difference.

3. Ask participants to work individually on an action plan for themselves, using Document 16.2, Action plan.

4. In the main group, ask participants to read out and share aspects of their action plans, including reviewing the learning gained from this exercise.

## Time required

1. Statements and responses take one hour.
2. Group discussion takes twenty minutes.
3. Action plans take twenty minutes.
4. Sharing action plans and review take twenty minutes.

Average total time: two hours.

## Resources and materials needed

1. Sufficient copies of Documents 16.1 and 16.2.
2. Sufficient space for groups to work undisturbed.
3. If required, a list of questions designed to raise any specific or relevant learning points.
4. Cards with different viewpoints relating to questions and statements.
5. Video camera and playback facilities (optional). If video is used you will need to make time for participants to view the material and to agree with them whether they wish to do this privately or within the group.

*Document 16.1 (Page 1 of 1)*

# Sample questions

1. People from the same country, location, etc. are all alike! How else can you explain why all Americans are loud or all Irish are dense or all Scots are tightfisted?

    Do you agree or disagree with this statement?

2. When people have no regard for correct or acceptable standards of dress it follows that they have no regard for decent, law-abiding behaviour.

    Do you agree or disagree with this statement?

3. No two people are alike and everyone has something to offer: that's why we should always treat people as individuals.

    Do you agree or disagree with this statement?

4. It's acceptable to employ women, black people and people with disabilities in jobs which require very little skill or intelligence, but they should not be promoted into positions of power because they don't know how to handle it.

    Do you agree or disagree with this statement?

5. People are entitled to their own views and opinions.

    Do you agree or disagree with this statement?

6. We say 'we shouldn't judge a book by its cover' and yet many people are judged on first impressions.

    Do you agree or disagree with this statement?

7. When things are going well and we're achieving results it doesn't make sense for people to keep suggesting new ideas.

    Do you agree or disagree with this statement?

Reproduced from *Facilitating Change: Ready-to-use training materials for the manager* by Barry Fletcher, Gower, Aldershot

*Document 16.2 (Page 1 of 2)*

# Action plan

1. What did I learn about myself and how I value people?

2. How happy do I feel about this discovery?

3. What changes do I need to make in order to alter my views on the value of people?

    (a) Over the next one to two weeks

Reproduced from *Facilitating Change: Ready-to-use training materials for the manager* by Barry Fletcher, Gower, Aldershot

*Document 16.2 (Page 2 of 2)*

    (b)    Over the next three to four weeks

    (c)    Over the next two to three months

4.    How can I do this and who can help me?

# 17

# Discovering ways of helping and influencing others

Effective teamwork relies on team members being influenced and those same team members being prepared to be influenced. There is no unique way to help or influence others and strategies which work for one person or situation may not work in another context.

This group activity provides participants with the opportunity to share and compare their different techniques as a means of discovering new ways for the future.

## Benefits

Participants undertaking this activity can expect to:

- recognize the benefits of using small groups for generating ideas;
- analyse the strategies they use currently to help and influence other people;
- explore alternative strategies for future use.

## Suitable for

This activity will help people who feel they have a limited repertoire of influencing and helping techniques. It will be of value to those who wish to discover and understand the techniques employed by other people.

*Facilitating Change*

## What to do

1. Divide participants into groups of three to six (maximum). Ask each group to elect one member to record the ideas. Each group should hold a brainstorming session following the sequence below:

    (a) Read out or display on a flipchart a prepared statement and ask the groups to brainstorm the 'positive' aspects of the statement. Some examples of statements which you could use are:

    - You can't teach an old dog new tricks.
    - The only effective way to help someone is to tell them what to do.
    - By law we should help each other.
    - Influence is always a good thing.

    (b) Ask groups to brainstorm the 'negative' aspects of the statement.

    (c) Ask groups to brainstorm the 'interesting' aspects of the statement.

    (d) In turn, ask each group to read out one of its positive aspects until all these have been shared. This process is then repeated for the negative and interesting aspects. (*Note:* there is no need to record these ideas collectively unless you feel they will be of particular value later.)

    Repeat the sequence for each of the prepared statements (these can be lighthearted at first and then become more serious or specific). The sequence need not be repeated more than three or four times as the aim of this part of the exercise is to highlight the increased range of ideas which can be generated from more than one person. You may wish to discuss the value of small-group work for generating ideas or may simply wish to mention this before moving on to the next stage.

2. Using Document 17.1, Helping and influencing strategies used in the past, ask participants individually to consider when and how they have helped or influenced people in the past.

3. Divide participants into small groups (threes and fours) and ask them to share each other's findings and discuss the positive, negative and interesting aspects of each example, recording these on a flipchart.

4. Bring participants together and ask each group to share its responses to Step 3. Encourage a review of the exercise, concentrating on the key learning points, and particularly how participants could adapt and use

*Discovering ways of helping and influencing others*

their learning in the future to develop new strategies for helping or influencing others.

5. Distribute Document 17.2, New strategies for helping or influencing others, and ask participants individually to list strategies they have discovered as a result of the exercise.

6. Back in the main group, ask participants to state two of the strategies from their lists which are new to them and which they are prepared to try in the future. Encourage each person to describe in detail how they might apply one of these two strategies. Invite questioning and discussion between participants to achieve clarity.

## Time required

1. Brainstorming responses to prepared statements takes thirty to forty minutes.
2. Completing Document 17.1 individually takes fifteen to twenty minutes.
3. Sharing and recording in groups takes twenty to thirty minutes.
4. Sharing responses and key learning points in the main group takes twenty to thirty minutes.
5. Completing Document 17.2 individually takes fifteen to twenty minutes.
6. Moving towards action, in the main group, takes forty-five minutes to one hour.

Average total time: three hours (including a short break).

## Resources and materials needed

1. Sufficient copies of Documents 17.1 and 17.2.
2. Prepared statements for Step 1.
3. Flipcharts, paper and pens.
4. Sufficient rooms and space to give participants a degree of privacy.

*Document 17.1 (Page 1 of 1)*

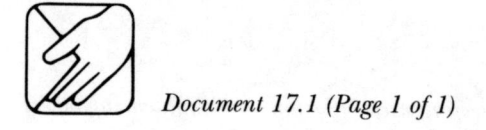

# Helping and influencing strategies used in the past

1. Under what circumstances have I chosen to help or influence other people?

2. In what ways have I helped or influenced others?

3. What went well and why?

4. What went wrong and why?

5. What other options could I have used?

Reproduced from *Facilitating Change: Ready-to-use training materials for the manager* by Barry Fletcher, Gower, Aldershot

*Document 17.2 (Page 1 of 1)*

# New strategies for helping or influencing others

| Options discovered | Positive aspects | Negative aspects | Interesting aspects |
|---|---|---|---|
|   |   |   |   |

Reproduced from *Facilitating Change: Ready-to-use training materials for the manager*
by Barry Fletcher, Gower, Aldershot

# 18

# Triggering my ability to influence others

*Lord, grant me the courage to change those things that need to be changed, the strength to endure those things that cannot be changed and the wisdom to know the difference.*
(Prayer attributed to St Francis)

All of us have been influenced, and have influenced others, both consciously and unconsciously. There are benefits to be gained from raising our understanding of how influence works.

This group activity considers the skills, qualities and abilities that are needed to influence others, and explores ways in which these can be 'triggered' in order to influence people and situations more effectively in the future.

## Benefits

Participants undertaking this activity can expect to:

- identify skills and qualities which they need to influence others;
- recognize the positive and negative aspects of influence;
- identify strategies for developing their capacity to influence others.

## Suitable for

This activity can be used by anyone who feels a need to influence others more effectively, for example, by people trying to introduce different ways of working or hoping to influence policies and practices. It will be of value to those who wish to discover and understand different influencing techniques employed by other people.

*Facilitating Change*

## What to do

You will need to be aware of the negative and positive aspects of influencing and be able to help people explore these issues in a safe, realistic way. If not handled well this activity could be seen to be encouraging people to manipulate others.

1. Ask the participants to choose two people they feel have greatly influenced them, one in favourable ways and the other unfavourably. These could be famous people, for example, a politician, writer, film star, or someone close to them, such as a parent, partner, workmate, friend. Next ask participants to brainstorm the qualities, skills and behaviours demonstrated by the people who influenced them favourably, for example encouragement, support, setting an example, challenging.

    Repeat the brainstorming exercise for those who influenced them unfavourably to arrive at another list of qualities, for example fear, power, coercion, threat.

    Encourage the group to discuss the differences and similarities displayed by both types and what key messages are emerging about influence.

2. Distribute Document 18.1, My spheres of influence matrix, and allow fifteen minutes for individuals to complete this.

3. Divide participants into small groups with a brief to discuss and share situations when they succeeded in influencing and how it felt. Also cover situations when they failed to influence and how that felt. Ask each group to record on a flipchart common thoughts and feelings from successful and failed influencing situations.

    Bring participants together and ask each group to report back on the discussions, using their flipcharts. Follow this with a discussion on common areas and sharing of key learning gained from this exercise.

4. Encourage the group to produce a checklist of dos and don'ts of influencing, together with any other key conclusions drawn from the activity. You may wish to have the list reproduced as a handout for the participants.

## Time required

1. Identifying influential people, brainstorming and discussion takes thirty to forty-five minutes.

2. Completing Document 18.1 individually takes fifteen minutes.

3. Sharing situations and discussion takes forty-five minutes to one hour.

4. Producing influencing checklist and conclusions takes twenty to thirty minutes.

Average total time: two hours and ten minutes.

## Resources and materials needed

1. Sufficient copies of Document 18.1.
2. Flipcharts and pens.
3. Sufficient rooms for groups to work in undisturbed.

*Document 18.1 (Page 1 of 1)*

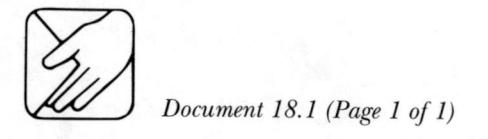

# My spheres of influence matrix

|  | My family/friends (the people around me) | My work colleagues (the people where I work) | Others (people in the world around me) |
|---|---|---|---|
| **When I influence or have influenced** | | | |
| **How I influence or have influenced** | | | |
| **Why I influence or have influenced** | | | |
| **Where I influence or have influenced** | | | |

Reproduced from *Facilitating Change: Ready-to-use training materials for the manager*
by Barry Fletcher, Gower, Aldershot

# 19

# Discovering new ways to learn

*'O! this learning, what a thing it is.'*
(from *The Taming of the Shrew*, William Shakespeare)

To many people, learning has connotations, often negative, of school, of classrooms and teachers, of examinations and the pressure to remember. This relatively fixed view can prevent us from discovering other, potentially more enjoyable and rewarding, ways of learning. Different people also have different learning preferences. Take an example of three people who learned about vehicle maintenance: Jane attended a course and took copious notes; David read books and articles avidly; while Matthew never made notes or read but asked many questions at his local garage.

This group activity, which can easily be adapted for individual use, enables participants to take stock of their learning habits and preferences. New ways of learning are identified and explored. Some of these may hold more interest and enjoyment for participants and may be more effective in meeting their learning needs.

## Benefits

Participants undertaking this activity can expect to:

- think about their previous learning experiences and identify their preferences so far;
- discover, and become more open to, new ways of learning;
- commit themselves to trying at least one new method of learning.

*Facilitating Change*

## Suitable for

This activity is suitable for most people in encouraging them to widen their view of learning methods. Used within a team it will enable members to tap into learning approaches which have proved successful for their colleagues.

The activity will be of value to anyone involved in the training and development of others, for example managers, mentors, supervisors, trainers and instructors.

## What to do

Before the activity, you may wish to familiarize yourself with the learning methods, materials, equipment and resources available to you and your staff. These can be described and made available for demonstration during the activity. For preparatory reading on learning styles and preferences the work of Honey and Mumford* is recommended.

1. After a brief introduction, give each participant a copy of Document 19.1, Traditional ways of learning – review, and allow about thirty minutes for completion, either individually or in pairs. Obtain feedback and encourage discussion on the points raised; it may help to record key points on a flipchart.

2. Divide participants into groups of three or four, and ask them to discuss and record their responses to the following (you may wish to write these on a flipchart before the session):

    (a) learning methods which we use most frequently;

    (b) learning methods we have not yet tried (this may be developed by brainstorming);

    (c) which of the methods listed in (a) and (b) would we as individuals like to try out on our next learning experience?

    Bring participants together and ask groups to share their findings.

3. Distribute Document 19.2, New learning technologies/techniques – quiz, and invite participants to complete this in their groups.

    When all groups have completed the quiz, bring participants together and distribute Document 19.3 which gives answers. Discuss the various techniques, demonstrating where possible, and encourage participants to state their interest in particular methods.

---

*P. Honey and A. Mumford, *The Manual of Learning Styles* (1986); *Using your Learning Styles* (1986); *The Opportunist Learner* (1990); *The Manual of Learning Opportunities* (1990).

4. Distribute Document 19.4, Application of new learning methods, for completing individually or in pairs.

5. Back in the main group, ask participants to announce their intentions, concentrating on those factors which will increase the likelihood of success. Clarify arrangements for support and monitoring. Review participants' learning from the activity.

## Time required

1. Introduction and completing Document 19.1 takes forty to fifty minutes.

2. Discovering new methods takes thirty to forty minutes.

3. Completing Document 19.2 and demonstrations take thirty to ninety minutes.

4. Completing Document 19.3 takes twenty to thirty minutes.

5. Sharing intentions and reviewing takes fifteen to thirty minutes.

Average total time: three hours.

## Resources and materials needed

1. Sufficient copies of Documents 19.1, 19.2, 19.3 and 19.4.

2. Sufficient space for groups to work uninterrupted.

3. Flipchart, paper and pens.

4. Equipment, tools and materials for demonstration purposes during Step 3.

*Document 19.1 (Page 1 of 1)*

# Traditional ways of learning – review

The aim of this exercise is to enable you to review the ways in which you have typically learned in the past (as a child, as an adult) and for you to recall those particular ways of learning that you enjoyed the most.

1. How did you learn as a child? (Consider pre-school, school, outside of school – games, hobbies, etc.)

2. How did you learn as an adult? (Consider learning methods at work (job specific), college, home/private life (learning to drive, cooking, DIY, looking after children, etc.).)

3. Reflecting on the ways you have learned in the past, which method did you enjoy most of all?

Document 19.2 (Page 1 of 2)

# New learning technologies/techniques – quiz

Complete the word/s appropriate to the description or clue. In the column to the right indicate whether you have used that method of learning:

| Words to be completed | Description/clue | O = often<br>S = sometimes<br>N = never |
|---|---|---|
| (1) _ _ _ _ _ _ T E _<br>_ _ _ E D<br>_ _ _ I _ I _ _ | Provides an immediate response to what the learner is doing. It is very good for less able learners and is stimulating to able learners. It has infinite patience and can be fairly expensive. It is often difficult to see the whole programme quickly. | |
| (2) _ _ E _<br>_ E _ _ N _ _ _ | Provides learning at a convenient time and place (in a location to suit) and at a rate which is neither hurried nor boring. It engages the learner in activity, not just passive listening and viewing, and it moves along in logical steps, building confidence and competence. It continually tests the user's understanding, giving extra help where needed and ensuring that new knowledge and skills are consolidated. It uses a variety of media from print to computer software and is delivered in a variety of ways from TV to small group and individual tutorials. | |
| (3) _ _ T _ _ A _ _ _ _ E<br>_ I _ _ _ | Is very responsive and realistic. It allows a wide range of responses by the learner. It is becoming less expensive and has an increasing number of standard packages coming onto the market. | |

Place a tick at the side of any of the above which you would like to try. Make a point of finding out more about that technology or technique.

Reproduced from *Facilitating Change: Ready-to-use training materials for the manager* by Barry Fletcher, Gower, Aldershot

Document 19.2 (Page 2 of 2)

| | Words to be completed | Description/clue | O = often<br>S = sometimes<br>N = never |
|---|---|---|---|
| (4) | – C – I – –<br>– – A – – – N – | An approach to management development based on doing the thing and not on abstract theories. | |
| (5) | – – C E – – – A – – –<br>– – – R – – – – | Utilizes a combination of learning methods to speed up the rate of learning, including relaxation techniques, 'baroque' background music and affirmation cards. | |
| (6) | – U – – O – –<br>– – – I – – – – | Uses a better, fresher and more invigorating environment in which to develop skills. | |
| (7) | – – – D<br>– – P – | Develops a whole range of connected ideas from a central thought on a single sheet of paper. It is ideal for quick recall. | |
| (8) | – I – U – – I – – – I – – | Uses the 'mind's eye' to practise. | |
| (9) | – – A – – – N –<br>– I – – L E – | Developed from a quality idea and involves voluntary participants with a common learning aim. | |
| (10) | – – – – O R – – – | Makes use of a wise counsellor to develop knowledge and skills by a combination of watching, doing and discussing with quick feedback. | |
| (11) | – – – A – – A – –<br>– – – I – A – – | Allows learning to start while others are just getting out of bed, and fills the stomach in the process. | |
| (12) | – E – – – – – – – T | Enables you to learn and reinforce skills while helping another department, team, or possibly another organization. | |

Place a tick at the side of any of the above which you would like to try. Make a point of finding out more about that technology or technique.

Reproduced from *Facilitating Change: Ready-to-use training materials for the manager* by Barry Fletcher, Gower, Aldershot

*Document 19.3 (Page 1 of 1)*

# New learning technologies/techniques – answer sheet

1. Computer based training.
2. Open learning.
3. Interactive video.
4. Action learning.
5. Accelerated learning
6. Outdoor training.
7. Mind maps.
8. Visualization.
9. Learning circles.
10. Mentoring.
11. Breakfast seminars.
12. Secondment.

Reproduced from *Facilitating Change: Ready-to-use training materials for the manager* by Barry Fletcher, Gower, Aldershot

*Document 19.4 (Page 1 of 1)*

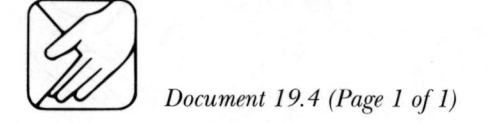

# Application of new learning methods

Either individually or in pairs, carry out the following tasks:

(a) Choose a specific learning need you have, for example:

- I would like to be able to ...
- I am having difficulty with ...
- It would help me if I could ...
- I want to become more skilled at ...

(b) Outline the way you would *normally* tackle this need.

(c) Outline the way you will *now* approach this need, based on the discussions and thoughts generated in the activity so far.

(d) Compare outlines (b) and (c), considering:

- Likely problems and means of overcoming these.
- Who else may be able to assist?
- The necessary resources (time, materials, etc.).
- Likely benefits.

# 20

# Removing the blinkers

Innovation, creativity and the generation of new ideas, the ingredients for continuous improvement, can be thwarted by fixed views and opinions.

This group activity, which can easily be adapted for individual use, enables participants to identify areas at work to which they may currently take a blinkered or narrow viewpoint. These insights can bring open-mindedness, thereby increasing the prospects for productive change.

## Benefits

Participants undertaking this activity can expect to:

- identify areas within which they may have a blinkered or narrow viewpoint;
- assess the extent to which they have become blinkered;
- develop their own action plan for change.

## Suitable for

This activity can be valuable within a team or group where ideas are not flowing, where there may be a feeling of being stuck, where there may be resistance to change from some members. It must be used sensitively if staff hold fixed views and opinions when there is a need for more flexibility in the future.

*Facilitating Change*

## What to do

The questionnaire and profile address a number of key areas at work and provide participants with data to increase their self-awareness. The six areas covered are A, People; B, Time – effort – motivation; C, Safety; D, Quality; E, Self-development and F, Change.

The questionnaire is designed with six statements for each of these six areas. Participants mark their level of agreement for each statement on the scale alongside. All statements on the questionnaire are randomly listed and answers are regrouped under the six areas when the profile assessment sheet is completed.

This activity is potentially emotive for some participants and you can do much to encourage support and constructive feedback. Encouraging open and frank discussion on potentially blinkered areas should stimulate participants to rethink their position and to consider some changes.

1. Distribute Document 20.1, RTB profile questionnaire, and ask each participant to complete it individually, allowing thirty to forty minutes.

2. After everyone is finished, distribute Document 20.2, RTB score sheet, for participants to complete. This should take about twenty minutes, but be prepared to give guidance on the scoring process.

3. Divide participants into groups of three to five with the following brief:

    (a) Discuss each profile and the extent to which these correspond with group members' perceptions of each other.

    (b) Discuss the potential uses of the profiles for broadening attitudes at work.

    (c) Identify options for eliminating or reducing blinkered areas (i.e. the lower scores on the profile).

    Bring participants together and allow time for findings to be fed back and discussed.

4. Encourage each participant to produce a personal action plan which takes into account their profile and the information gained from Step 3.

5. In the main group encourage participants to share their personal action plans and to describe at least two behaviours to which they are committed as a result of completing the activity.

## Time required

1. Completing Document 20.1 takes thirty to forty minutes.

2. Scoring takes twenty minutes.

3. Discussion in groups and feedback take forty-five to sixty minutes.

4. Preparing personal action plans takes twenty minutes.

5. Review and sharing commitments to change take twenty to thirty minutes.

Average total time: two hours thirty minutes.

## Resources and materials needed

1. Sufficient copies of Documents 20.1 and 20.2.

2. Sufficient space for participants to work undisturbed.

3. Coloured pens, highlighter pens, flipcharts and paper.

*Document 20.1 (Page 1 of 4)*

# RTB profile questionnaire

For each of the following statements circle one of the numbers on the scale to show your level of agreement.

Key:  1 = strongly agree
      2 = agree
      3 = slightly agree
      4 = neither agree nor disagree
      5 = slightly disagree
      6 = disagree
      7 = strongly disagree

| | | |
|---|---|---|
| 1. | Suggestion schemes are a great idea, they generate many useful and practical solutions | 1  2  3  4  5  6  7 |
| 2. | Taking work home regularly each night shows a sense of keenness and always indicates an efficient and effective worker | 1  2  3  4  5  6  7 |
| 3. | I cannot improve upon the quality of my work if my suppliers' quality is bad | 1  2  3  4  5  6  7 |
| 4. | Firms which allow employees to spend the first ten minutes of each day 'chit-chatting' are losing around five days per employee per year – they're bound to be less efficient than those who disallow such practice | 1  2  3  4  5  6  7 |
| 5. | If I were paid more I would work harder | 1  2  3  4  5  6  7 |
| 6. | In a time of recession, men should be given priority over women for available jobs | 1  2  3  4  5  6  7 |
| 7. | I don't go out of my way to welcome newcomers. I let them settle in first and then if they're my 'type' I'll make contact with them | 1  2  3  4  5  6  7 |
| 8. | Our section could improve on quality without it costing any money | 1  2  3  4  5  6  7 |

Reproduced from *Facilitating Change: Ready-to-use training materials for the manager*
by Barry Fletcher, Gower, Aldershot

| 9. | Improving our quality doesn't need to slow down the job | 1 2 3 4 5 6 7 |
|---|---|---|
| 10. | Our quality has always been good but these days people expect more for less | 1 2 3 4 5 6 7 |
| 11. | Learning is now easier than ever – with so many different ways to learn it can even be fun | 1 2 3 4 5 6 7 |
| 12. | Change is a fact of life, it's inevitable and we've always had it. It's just that these days it happens quicker | 1 2 3 4 5 6 7 |
| 13. | When I find a good method I stick to it regardless – there's no point in changing a good thing | 1 2 3 4 5 6 7 |
| 14. | Learning is a chore – it's the same old routine of watching, listening, reading and memorizing | 1 2 3 4 5 6 7 |
| 15. | I can help to improve quality provided people 'listen' to what I have to say | 1 2 3 4 5 6 7 |
| 16. | Accident-prone people should be dismissed. They are a hazard to all | 1 2 3 4 5 6 7 |
| 17. | I am not responsible for my neighbours' repeatedly careless acts | 1 2 3 4 5 6 7 |
| 18. | If I see a hazard I try to eliminate it, or I always report it | 1 2 3 4 5 6 7 |
| 19. | Improving safety always costs money so it's bound to take a low priority | 1 2 3 4 5 6 7 |
| 20. | The more often people are made aware of safety hazards the greater the chance we have of reducing accidents | 1 2 3 4 5 6 7 |

Reproduced from *Facilitating Change: Ready-to-use training materials for the manager*
by Barry Fletcher, Gower, Aldershot

Document 20.1 (Page 3 of 4)

Key:  1 = strongly agree
      2 = agree
      3 = slightly agree
      4 = neither agree nor disagree
      5 = slightly disagree
      6 = disagree
      7 = strongly disagree

| 21. | I'm never too busy to take lunch | 1 2 3 4 5 6 7 |
|---|---|---|
| 22. | Everyone goes through a bad patch occasionally so we should watch for the signs and help support others when it happens | 1 2 3 4 5 6 7 |
| 23. | Organizations should take special measures to deal with disadvantaged groups – we cannot expect the government to do it all | 1 2 3 4 5 6 7 |
| 24. | We could improve quality quickly if they paid us more | 1 2 3 4 5 6 7 |
| 25. | They're always bringing in new ideas and methods before you've had the chance to become comfortable with the old. Why can't they just let things settle for a while? | 1 2 3 4 5 6 7 |
| 26. | Change can be a good thing – it often brings challenges and excitement: it's like a breath of fresh air | 1 2 3 4 5 6 7 |
| 27. | Continuous learning not only benefits my employer it also makes me a richer, fuller person | 1 2 3 4 5 6 7 |
| 28. | Self-development is a way of life – it's as important as eating and sleeping | 1 2 3 4 5 6 7 |
| 29. | Only stiffer laws and penalties will stop accidents happening | 1 2 3 4 5 6 7 |
| 30. | Working harder only benefits the firm – it doesn't give me any greater reward | 1 2 3 4 5 6 7 |

Reproduced from *Facilitating Change: Ready-to-use training materials for the manager*
by Barry Fletcher, Gower, Aldershot

| | | |
|---|---|---|
| 31. | I don't give my ideas away freely, someone will always take advantage and claim the credit | 1  2  3  4  5  6  7 |
| 32. | I nearly always complete the tasks I set out to achieve in the average working day | 1  2  3  4  5  6  7 |
| 33. | Learning new career skills should always be done in work time not mine | 1  2  3  4  5  6  7 |
| 34. | The organization is responsible for my training – I expect them to tell me what I need to learn | 1  2  3  4  5  6  7 |
| 35. | Older workers will not adapt to new ideas, they get stuck in their ways – it's always the young ones who take the lead | 1  2  3  4  5  6  7 |
| 36. | I often move things around at my workplace, it gives the place a new freshness. | 1  2  3  4  5  6  7 |

Reproduced from *Facilitating Change: Ready-to-use training materials for the manager* by Barry Fletcher, Gower, Aldershot

*Document 20.2 (Page 1 of 2)*

# RTB score sheet

1. For each statement number, in turn, circle the score given appropriate to your scale number chosen.

2. Transfer your circled score to the appropriate blank column.

| Statement number | Scale number 1 | 2 | 3 | 4 | 5 | 6 | 7 | A | B | C | D | E | F |
|---|---|---|---|---|---|---|---|---|---|---|---|---|---|
| 1 | 6 | 5 | 4 | 3 | 2 | 1 | 0 |   | X | X | X | X | X |
| 2 | 0 | 1 | 2 | 3 | 4 | 5 | 6 | X |   | X | X | X | X |
| 3 | 0 | 1 | 2 | 3 | 4 | 5 | 6 | X | X | X |   | X | X |
| 4 | 0 | 1 | 2 | 3 | 4 | 5 | 6 | X |   | X | X | X | X |
| 5 | 0 | 1 | 2 | 3 | 4 | 5 | 6 | X |   | X | X | X | X |
| 6 | 0 | 1 | 2 | 3 | 4 | 5 | 6 |   | X | X | X | X | X |
| 7 | 0 | 1 | 2 | 3 | 4 | 5 | 6 |   | X | X | X | X | X |
| 8 | 6 | 5 | 4 | 3 | 2 | 1 | 0 | X | X | X |   | X | X |
| 9 | 6 | 5 | 4 | 3 | 2 | 1 | 0 | X | X | X |   | X | X |
| 10 | 0 | 1 | 2 | 3 | 4 | 5 | 6 | X | X | X |   | X | X |
| 11 | 6 | 5 | 4 | 3 | 2 | 1 | 0 | X | X | X | X |   | X |
| 12 | 6 | 5 | 4 | 3 | 2 | 1 | 0 | X | X | X | X | X |   |
| 13 | 0 | 1 | 2 | 3 | 4 | 5 | 6 | X | X | X | X | X |   |
| 14 | 0 | 1 | 2 | 3 | 4 | 5 | 6 | X | X | X | X |   | X |
| 15 | 6 | 5 | 4 | 3 | 2 | 1 | 0 | X | X | X |   | X | X |
| 16 | 0 | 1 | 2 | 3 | 4 | 5 | 6 | X | X |   | X | X | X |
| 17 | 0 | 1 | 2 | 3 | 4 | 5 | 6 | X | X |   | X | X | X |
| 18 | 6 | 5 | 4 | 3 | 2 | 1 | 0 | X | X |   | X | X | X |
| 19 | 0 | 1 | 2 | 3 | 4 | 5 | 6 | X | X |   | X | X | X |
| 20 | 6 | 5 | 4 | 3 | 2 | 1 | 0 | X | X |   | X | X | X |
| 21 | 6 | 5 | 4 | 3 | 2 | 1 | 0 | X |   | X | X | X | X |
| 22 | 6 | 5 | 4 | 3 | 2 | 1 | 0 |   | X | X | X | X | X |
| 23 | 6 | 5 | 4 | 3 | 2 | 1 | 0 |   | X | X | X | X | X |
| 24 | 0 | 1 | 2 | 3 | 4 | 5 | 6 | X | X | X |   | X | X |
| 25 | 0 | 1 | 2 | 3 | 4 | 5 | 6 | X | X | X | X | X |   |
| 26 | 6 | 5 | 4 | 3 | 2 | 1 | 0 | X | X | X | X | X |   |
| 27 | 6 | 5 | 4 | 3 | 2 | 1 | 0 | X | X | X | X |   | X |
| 28 | 6 | 5 | 4 | 3 | 2 | 1 | 0 | X | X | X | X |   | X |
| 29 | 0 | 1 | 2 | 3 | 4 | 5 | 6 | X | X |   | X | X | X |
| 30 | 0 | 1 | 2 | 3 | 4 | 5 | 6 | X |   | X | X | X | X |
| 31 | 0 | 1 | 2 | 3 | 4 | 5 | 6 |   | X | X | X | X | X |
| 32 | 6 | 5 | 4 | 3 | 2 | 1 | 0 | X |   | X | X | X | X |
| 33 | 0 | 1 | 2 | 3 | 4 | 5 | 6 | X | X | X | X |   | X |
| 34 | 0 | 1 | 2 | 3 | 4 | 5 | 6 | X | X | X | X |   | X |
| 35 | 0 | 1 | 2 | 3 | 4 | 5 | 6 | X | X | X | X | X |   |
| 36 | 6 | 5 | 4 | 3 | 2 | 1 | 0 | X | X | X | X | X |   |

3. Total each column →

4. Change your scores to percentages (divide by 36 and multiply by 100). For example, → % % % % % %
   $$\frac{\text{column total} \times 100}{36}$$

*Reproduced from Facilitating Change: Ready-to-use training materials for the manager by Barry Fletcher, Gower, Aldershot*

*Document 20.2 (Page 2 of 2)*

## Your profile

5. Mark each percentage score, on the appropriate line of the profile wheel.

6. Join up the marks to give your profile.

7. Colour in the area (preferably with a highlighter pen) between the profile line and the outer circle.

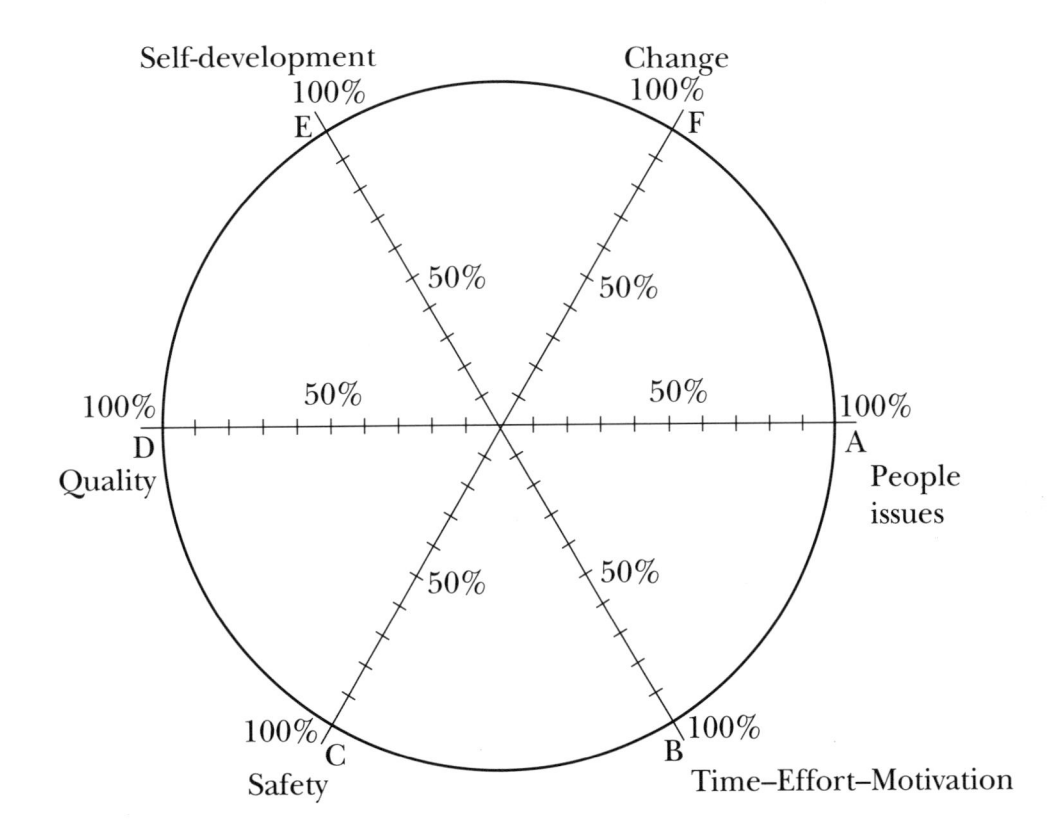

183

Reproduced from *Facilitating Change: Ready-to-use training materials for the manager* by Barry Fletcher, Gower, Aldershot

# 21

# Understanding reactions to change

*'To meet the demands of the fast-changing competitive scene, we must simply learn to love change as much as we have hated it in the past.'*
(Tom Peters, *Thriving on Chaos*, Pan/Macmillan, 1987)

This group activity provides opportunities for staff to consider the process of organizational change and to reflect on ways of improving acceptance of it. A case study is used to help participants think about and discuss strategies for dealing with reactions to organizational change.

## Benefits

Participants undertaking this activity can expect to:

- learn a structured approach to identifying, in advance, the likely reactions to an organizational change;
- analyse how which parts of the change generate different reactions;
- plan how to minimize resistance to organizational change using a case study;
- transfer the lessons from the case study to their own workplace, thereby becoming better able to anticipate the consequences of change.

## Suitable for

This activity will be of value to anyone who wishes to raise their understanding of change and teams and groups who may be facing the prospect of significant organizational change.

*Facilitating Change*

## What to do

In preparation you may wish to consult the Introduction to this manual and the background notes to this activity, Document 21.1. As part of the group's preparation you may choose to send each participant Document 21.1, together with copies of the case study, Document 21.4, one to two weeks before the session.

1. Give a brief introduction and overview of the subject.

2. Give a copy of Document 21.2, Managing change – evaluation form, to each participant and briefly explain its use. That is, it is an analytical instrument which can be used to assist in the evaluation of a specific organizational change with the aim of developing a strategy for acceptance.

    As an option, participants can work through the steps in Document 21.3, using the example of a new incentive scheme, to increase their understanding of the use of the evaluation form. At each stage ask participants to contribute their own views, share them with colleagues and ask questions before moving on.

3. Distribute Document 21.4, Case study – Choice Manufacturing. Divide participants into groups of three to five and ask each group to proceed through the following stages:

    (a) Analyse the case study with the aid of Document 21.2.

    (b) Decide on a strategy aimed at minimizing resistance to the change.

    (c) Prepare to report on your chosen strategy.

4. Allow time for groups to present their strategies to the main group. Encourage discussion, challenges and questions.

5. In the main group hold a learning review session, addressing questions such as:

    - How valuable is this structured approach?
    - Which current and anticipated changes lend themselves to this approach?
    - What obstacles are anticipated in using this approach and how could they be circumvented?

Conclude by asking participants to give examples of how, where and when they intend to use this approach in the near future.

## Time required

1. The introduction and overview take twenty to thirty minutes.
2. Explaining Document 21.2 takes ten minutes and working through the example in Document 21.3 (optional) takes thirty to forty minutes.
3. Strategy choice takes forty-five to sixty minutes.
4. Presentations and discussion take thirty minutes.
5. The learning review and deciding practical applications take thirty minutes.

Average total time: three hours (includes working through example).

## Resources and materials needed

1. Sufficient copies of Documents 21.1, 21.2, 21.3 and 21.4.
2. Sufficient space for groups to work undisturbed.
3. Flipchart, paper, OHP, acetates and pens for presentations.

Document 21.1 (Page 1 of 4)

# Understanding reaction to change – background notes

People in organizations are often faced with the challenge of introducing change. This can be:

(a) *self-created* – the idea, the resources and the authority to make it happen, or

(b) *imposed* – variable influence plus reponsibility for implementing the change with minimum disruption to operations.

The change could be large scale and even drastic, as in the case of company merger or takeover with possible redundancies. At the other extreme, the change could be subtle or slight, as in the case of a minor change to a job description.

## TYPICAL CHANGE SITUATIONS

- Merged companies, sections and departments.
- Introduction of new technology.
- Introduction of new systems, procedures, practices, policies.
- Change in corporate structure.
- Increased levels of responsibility.
- Changes in duties.
- Increased levels of work or work pressure.
- Reductions in rewards, benefits and remuneration in real terms.

Reactions to such changes can be considered as:

(a) *positive* – general agreement and acceptance by all concerned together with their full commitment to making it happen, or

(b) *negative* – resistance to the change for whatever reason.

Those wishing to bring about the change will be aiming to achieve positive reactions from others. These may not come readily or easily, but with foresight and careful planning a satisfactory outcome is possible.

Reflecting for a moment on the undesirable outcome, that is negative reactions or resistance from others, common causes are:

Reproduced from *Facilitating Change: Ready-to-use training materials for the manager* by Barry Fletcher, Gower, Aldershot

- Fear of the unknown.
- Sudden announcements of change, without warning.
- Being pressurized into situations where unforeseen difficulties may arise.
- Many subtle and gradual changes accumulating over a long period, each of which is insignificant in isolation but taken as a whole can build up to frustration and even anger.
- No net gain or reward perceived (possibly seen as a loss).

*SOME EFFECTS OF RESISTANCE*

- Drop in morale.
- Group unrest.
- Loss of productivity.
- Drop in quality standards.
- Refusal to cooperate.
- Industrial relations problems and unrest.
- Increased absenteeism.
- Deterioration in time-keeping standards.
- Increased aggression at meetings.

Such effects can become *key indicators* of a change being resisted. Reaction to change can be anything from absolute refusal to cooperate at one extreme to full acceptance and commitment at the other. There are shades of resistance in between, for example:

(a) *hidden resistance* – where the individual or group voices acceptance but quietly strives towards causing a failed outcome;

(b) *cautious acceptance* – acceptance without full commitment, plus readiness to revert to resistance should problems occur.

*Document 21.1 (Page 3 of 4)*

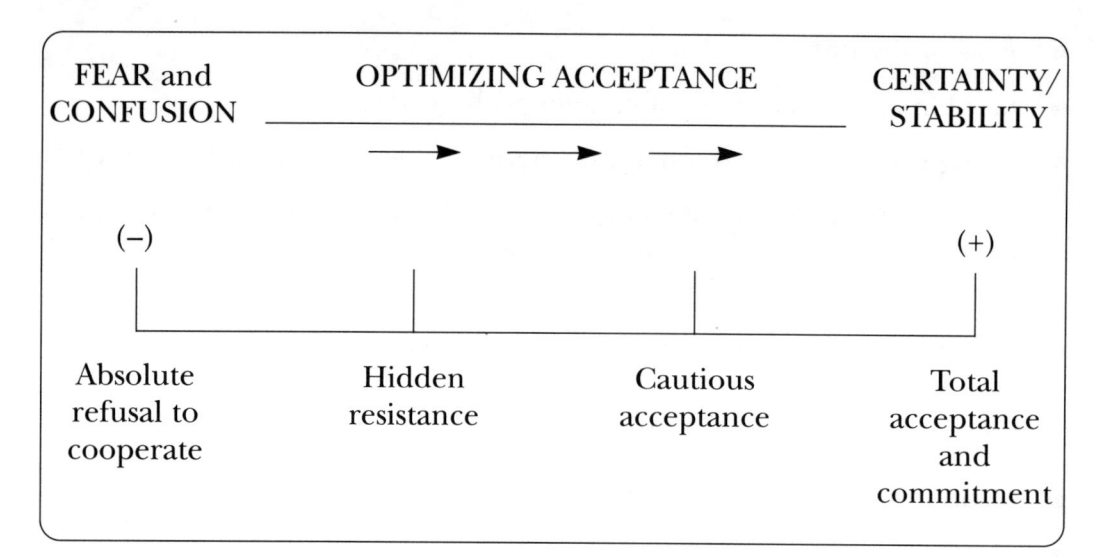

```
FEAR and           OPTIMIZING ACCEPTANCE            CERTAINTY/
CONFUSION          ─────────────────────            STABILITY
                      ──▶   ──▶   ──▶

   (−)                                                 (+)
    │           │            │              │
    │           │            │              │
 Absolute     Hidden       Cautious        Total
 refusal to   resistance   acceptance      acceptance
 cooperate                                 and
                                           commitment
```

**Scale of Reaction**

Whether the proposed change is imposed or self-created, a strategy will be required to optimize acceptance. There will be a gap between what is current and what is required. The aim is to close that gap as painlessly and effectively as possible.

*STRATEGY FOR HIGH ACCEPTANCE*

1. *Think* carefully and write down precisely the planned change.
2. *Consider* who will be most affected – directly and indirectly.
3. *Decide* what new skills and knowledge will be required for:

    - new machinery, procedures, systems
    - coping with related changes and tasks
    - coping with new working relationships.

4. *Determine* what existing knowledge can be used with this change.
5. *Decide* how best to communicate the change, for example:

    - Draft the change plan.
    - Discuss and clarify the purpose of the change with all concerned (may result in feedback showing likely reaction).
    - Seek suggestions but *do not* promise to follow them.
    - Make it clear that some people may already have the skills needed and that you may be soliciting their support.

Reproduced from *Facilitating Change: Ready-to-use training materials for the manager* by Barry Fletcher, Gower, Aldershot

*Document 21.1 (Page 4 of 4)*

- Use every opportunity to affirm the change via memos, update meetings, newsletters, project suggestion schemes, staff visits to other firms/exhibitions, circulation of journals and magazines, provision of books, videos, open-learning materials, etc.

- Design and communicate the training and coaching plan.

- Programme regular reviews.

6. *Establish* an 'acid test' for the change by asking yourself: 'How will I know that acceptance and commitment have been secured, and the change achieved'?

*Document 21.2 (Page 1 of 2)*

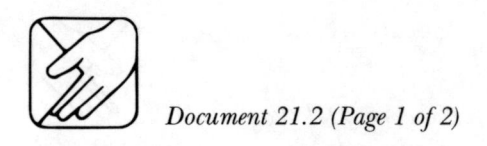

# Managing change – evaluation form

Complete the form below, using the instructions on the next sheet.

| a | The change: | | | | | | | | | | | | | | |
|---|---|---|---|---|---|---|---|---|---|---|---|---|---|---|---|
| b | Change element | c Value | d Scale of reaction A B C D | | | e Why resistance? | f Benefits of the change — To the organization | To the individual/group |

Reproduced from *Facilitating Change: Ready-to-use training materials for the manager* by Barry Fletcher, Gower, Aldershot

# Evaluation form – instructions for use

The letters relate to those which appear on the form.

*a*   Brief description of the change.

*b*   Write down the actions which need to be taken to close the 'gap' between what is current and what is wanted.

*c*   To indicate 'value' use the following:

   V = vital to success
   B = beneficial to quality of success
   N = neutral – makes no difference

*d*   Tick in the appropriate box:

   A = absolute refusal to cooperate
   B = hidden resistance
   C = cautious acceptance
   D = full acceptance and commitment.

*e–f*   Enter additional information to aid strategy formulation.

Use this evaluation to help you to formulate an outline strategy for success, as follows:

---

**Outline strategy for success**

Using the information from the form develop the key elements of a strategy for success. Consider:

- those affected (directly and indirectly)
- skills and knowledge required
- existing skills and knowledge which can be utilized
- how best to communicate the change.

*ACID TEST*

How will you know you have achieved success?

---

Reproduced from *Facilitating Change: Ready-to-use training materials for the manager* by Barry Fletcher, Gower, Aldershot

Document 21.3 (Page 1 of 2)

# Example of using change evaluation form

The following example of a new incentive scheme increases understanding of using the form in Document 21.2. The letters correspond to sections on the form.

(a) Write down in a *single statement* the desired change, for example:
'To install an incentive scheme based upon work measurement'.

(b) List those *key* change elements which will have to be actioned in order successfully to effect the change: that is, those actions which must be taken in order to close the gap between what is current and what is wanted.
For this example the following actions could be required:

- Engage work study practitioners.
- Carry out pilot studies using activity sampling.
- Decide on the priority order of departments to be studied.
- Study the range of jobs in each department.
- Establish the financial base of the incentive scheme.
- Set allowances for relaxation, contingency, etc.
- Set up a monitoring system.

(c) Judge the value for successful implementation of each element in turn using the following codes:

| | | |
|---|---|---|
| V | = Vital | The change cannot be effected without this being achieved. |
| B | = Beneficial | The change could be effected without this being achieved, but its absence will reduce the quality of the change as a whole. |
| N | = Neutral | Absence of this element will not affect the quality of the change. Use of this raises the question of whether it is 'key'. |

(d) Taking each change element in turn, indicate on the 'scale of reaction' the likely reaction of the target group, where:

Reproduced from *Facilitating Change: Ready-to-use training materials for the manager* by Barry Fletcher, Gower, Aldershot

*Document 21.3 (Page 2 of 2)*

    A = absolute refusal to cooperate

    B = hidden resistance

    C = cautious acceptance

    D = full acceptance and commitment

(e) If resistance is expected, briefly state why.

(f) List the main benefits to the organization, and to the individual or group, resulting from successful implementation of the change.

Having completed the form, examine the combined information and agree any key factors of which a strategy for successful implementation would need to take account.

To conclude, discuss the exercise and draw conclusions on:

- Your perceptions of the value of the form.
- Ease/difficulty of completing the form.
- Thoughts on applying the form to work situations.

Reproduced from *Facilitating Change: Ready-to-use training materials for the manager* by Barry Fletcher, Gower, Aldershot

Document 21.4 (Page 1 of 3)

# Case study – understanding reaction to change

Choice Manufacturing Co. Ltd., an expanding company servicing the nuclear power industry, has just acquired Magnetic Power Pumps Ltd, as part of its strategy of backward integration. Choice has been purchasing pumps from Magnetic for the past ten years.

The board of Choice has said publicly that there will be no forced redundancies which reflects the wishes of its shareholders. However, for economic reasons, the premises of Magnetic will be sold and all resources will be transferred to Choice's current site, all departments becoming fully integrated.

## The problem

You are the Design Director of Choice and have accepted the unanimous decision of your board fully to integrate the design department of Magnetic with your own.

## Background to the design department of Choice

The success of Choice is reflected in the high volume of work flowing through the design department. Despite offering above average conditions and salaries, recruitment of staff of the right calibre has been very difficult. This is expected to become even worse in the light of current demographic trends, particularly a severe decline in the number of school-leavers over the next five years.

The department has a staff of 60, 20 per cent of which are female. It is a young, highly motivated and professional team with only 5 per cent aged over 40; 60 per cent are between 25 and 35 with the remaining 35 per cent under the age of 25. All staff are highly qualified – each possessing, or studying for, an engineering degree. This stems from strict recruitment and training policies which specify minimum entry standards and encourage 'ongoing training for professional updating'.

Eighty-five per cent of all work in the department is carried out on computer aided design (CAD) equipment. The remainder is carried out manually to maintain some cover in the event of computer malfunction.

The open-plan office layout boasts smart, trendy furnishings and decor. The office is spacious and could house another 20 staff quite comfortably. General employment conditions include:

Reproduced from *Facilitating Change: Ready-to-use training materials for the manager* by Barry Fletcher, Gower, Aldershot

- structured salary scale linked to a job evaluation and merit scheme;
- 37-hour week with flexi-time, one hour lunch and no formal breaks;
- 33 days' annual leave with an extra five days after five years' continuous service;
- index-linked pension plan and free health insurance;
- uniforms (short, white cotton jackets) are compulsory;
- high-quality, heavily subsidized canteen: soft drinks available from vending machine within department;
- some work is structured through project teams with total versatility within each team.

Initial soundings have been taken and the feedback suggests integration will not present problems providing the 'newcomers' accept the conditions under which Choice staff currently work.

## Background to the design department of Magnetic

Magnetic staff had been taken completely by surprise at the takeover of their company and many now fear for their jobs as a result of rumours.

Magnetic was a traditional family firm – some would say 'Victorian' – which had built up a reputation for good design of a sturdy and reliable product.

The design department manager and a few of his more senior staff had occasionally visited Choice to liaise on design requirements. The manager, who is now taking early retirement as a result of the takeover, related the feelings of his 12 staff:

> There's an air of gloom due to this messy business. None of my men are happy, apart from the young lad (apprentice), who is very excited. They're all getting on a bit you see and all this talk about fancy computers and flexible working – not to mention regulation uniform – well it's all a bit much for them. You see they're from the old school; all they know is tee-square and pencil, not fancy computers. Give 'em a tee-square and pencil and they'll redesign the Universe! No, I think Choice has bitten off a bit more than it can chew with this one. You're going to have a right old job shipping my lads up there!

Of the 12 design staff at Magnetic, 11 are aged over 50 years and two of these are 61 and 62 years. The trainee draughtsman is aged 20 and currently studying for a Higher National Certificate. All staff were promoted from the shopfloor after serving traditional apprenticeships in engineering. Most

*Document 21.4 (Page 3 of 3)*

gained their qualifications by evening attendance, apart from the young man who attends by day-release.

General employment conditions include:

- individually negotiated salaries which tend to be about average for the industry, however the salaries of the two eldest are on a par with the project team leaders at Choice;
- 37-hour week (8 a.m. to 5 p.m. with an early finish on Fridays);
- 31 days' annual leave;
- basic pension plan but no health insurance;
- a 'homely' canteen;
- two 15-minute tea-breaks (staff providing own kettle, tea, etc.);
- dowdy looking, old-fashioned office with some staff occupying small adjacent offices often called the 'rabbit warren';
- training non-existent, except in the case of the apprentice, and an occasional seminar;
- all staff specialized in one of three separate functions (design, detail draughting, tracing).

# 22

# Identifying strategies for change

This activity uses three techniques which can help you and your staff to identify strategies for change. These are:

- *Option 1* – Examining the pros and cons of an issue.
- *Option 2* – Assessing my choices.
- *Option 3* – Positive and negative 'self-talk'.

## Benefits

The activity provides participants with a choice of strategies for addressing and managing change. Further outcomes are specified under each option.

## Suitable for

This activity can be used by anyone involved in:

- change at work, home etc.
- making decisions
- problem solving
- contracting or negotiating.

*Facilitating Change*

**Special note**

Where appropriate, guide notes are included within each option. Also included are notes on what to do, together with time and materials requirements. In this way, you are provided with maximum flexibility – any combination of the options can be used. The options are written for group use but each can be easily adapted for use by individuals. If you decide to use them with individuals, arrange an introductory briefing session followed by one or two further discussion and review meetings during the following two to three weeks.

Before using the options with members of your staff you could benefit from working through one or more of them yourself.

*Identifying strategies for change*

# OPTION 1: Examining the pros and cons of an issue

## Benefits

Participants undertaking this activity can expect to:

- identify the 'driving' and 'resisting' factors associated with a situation;
- explore the possible consequences of altering the driving or resisting factors;
- identify the next steps to be taken to change the situation;
- draw lessons from this method of planning change.

## What to do

1. Distribute Document 22.1, Examining the pros and cons of an issue, and ask participants to think of a current issue that affects us all, for example 'the greenhouse effect' or 'the misuse of drugs in our society'. Encourage the group to discuss the issue and identify the driving and resisting factors. Explore the consequences of increasing or reducing one or both of these factors and some of the strategies for achieving these changes.

2. Ask participants individually to think of any situations in their life or circumstances which they would like to change or are in the process of changing. From these situations, invite each participant to choose *one* to process further. Distribute Document 22.2, Driving/resisting factors, and allow time for individuals to record their thoughts.

3. In pairs, ask participants to share their responses to Document 22.2 and constructively challenge each other's thinking on the situation to be changed.
    (*Note:* If you are using this option on your own you are advised to discuss your thoughts with another person as this enables you to be clearer about your options.)

4. Review the key points of the exercise, for example by posing the following questions:

- How did you feel about the exercise?
- In what ways did the technique help/hinder your thinking?
- What were the main learning points for you?

*Facilitating Change*

- What lessons does this have for you in relation to ...?
- How can you further this approach?

Also ask participants to reflect on previous situations where they have adopted a strategy of increasing the driving factors without giving too much thought to understanding and reducing the resisting factors.

## Time required

1. The discussion takes twenty to thirty minutes.
2. Completing Document 22.2 takes twenty to thirty minutes.
3. Sharing in pairs takes fifteen to twenty minutes.
4. Group review takes fifteen to twenty minutes.

Average total time: one hour and thirty minutes.

## Resources and materials needed

1. Sufficient copies of Document 22.1 and 22.2.
2. Sufficient space for participants to work undisturbed.

# OPTION 2: Assessing my choices

## Benefits

Participants undertaking this activity can expect to:

- identify some of the choices open to them;
- explore which of their choices are most viable;
- develop their own action plan for implementing the change which they have chosen;
- draw lessons for themselves from this method of deciding what changes to make.

## What to do

1. Ask participants individually to spend a little time thinking about and writing down a situation they would like to change.

2. Divide participants into small groups of, say, four people, and ask each person to describe their chosen situation briefly. Using Document 22.3, Choices framework, each person can then talk through the range of choices open to them. The other group members are asked to challenge the person's thinking and if necessary help to look at the choices in a different light. (*Note:* It is important to stress that any challenge must be constructive and supportive and *not* negative and attacking.) Each person in the group should have about ten to fifteen minutes to explore their choices.

3. Individually, ask participants to prepare an action plan, using Document 22.4, for implementing their choice(s).

4. Review the exercise using the following questions:

    - How did you feel about the exercise?
    - In what ways did the technique help/hinder your thinking?
    - What were the main learning points for you?
    - What lessons does this have for you in relation to ...?
    - How can you further this approach?

*Facilitating Change*

## Time required

1. Deciding situations for change takes ten minutes.
2. Talking through choices using Document 22.3 takes forty minutes to one hour.
3. Completing Document 22.4, Action plan, takes ten to fifteen minutes.
4. Group review takes fifteen to twenty minutes.

Average total time: one hour forty minutes.

## Resources and materials needed

1. Sufficient copies of Documents 22.3 and 22.4.
2. Enough space/room for participants to work in privacy.

*Identifying strategies for change*

# OPTION 3: Positive/negative 'self-talk'

## Benefits

Participants undertaking this activity can expect to:

- realize how the way they talk to themselves influences the way they approach change;
- become more prepared to change the way they talk to themselves;
- increase the range of change about which they feel positive;
- become more committed and flexible in their stance towards change.

## What to do

1. Distribute Document 22.5, Positive/negative self-talk, and encourage comments and discussion.

2. Invite participants to think about, and write down examples of, their own self-talk. Some prompts may be necessary to help them, for example self-talk relating to:

   - my perceptions of myself
   - the standards I set myself
   - my approach to my work
   - the way I tackle problems and difficulties
   - the things I tell myself about other people's perceptions of me
   - the things I tell myself about my skills and abilities
   - what I say to myself about my achievements
   - what I tell myself about making mistakes and failing
   - what I tell myself about opportunities and career prospects
   - what I say to myself about my confidence.

   Ask participants to mark each of their self-talk statements as either 'P' (positive) or 'N' (negative).

3. Ask each participant to share at least one 'N' and one 'P' statement with the group. Use the group to help each person explore the consequences

*Facilitating Change*

of these sample statements and to practise rewording them and saying them out aloud. Continue with this stage until all participants have been involved.

4. Ask each participant to reconsider at least *three* of their negative self-talk statements and to reword these in more positive terms. Finally, encourage sharing of these in small groups or pairs and seek commitments from participants to use these 'new' self-talk statements in the future.

## Time required

1. Discussing self-talk using Document 22.5 takes fifteen to twenty minutes.
2. Considering and writing down statements takes twenty to thirty minutes.
3. Sharing and rewording statements takes thirty to fifty minutes.
4. Rewording, sharing and contracting in small groups takes twenty to thirty minutes.

Average total time: two hours.

## Resources and materials needed

1. Sufficient copies of Document 22.5.
2. Paper and pens.

# Examining the pros and cons of an issue

In every situation, there are factors, people, events and circumstances pushing *for* change – the *driving factors*. Likewise, in every situation there are factors, people, events and circumstances pushing *against* change – the *resisting factors*.

These factors push against each other continually, but the pressure is not always constant. It can vary according to the strength, commitment, determination or stubbornness of the people involved and can be affected by outside influences such as public opinion, changes in the law, changes in circumstances of the people involved, etc.

When we want to negotiate changes of any kind, we need to explore the driving and resisting factors as well as considering the issue from both sides. We need to explore and consider what effect applying some extra pressure in one area will have on the resisting pressures somewhere else. Conversely, by increasing our understanding of the resisting factors we may be able to engage in behaviours which reduce these, thus contributing to our desired change.

By being aware of these factors and using them positively, we can begin to develop strategies which will improve the quality and effectiveness of our negotiations for change.

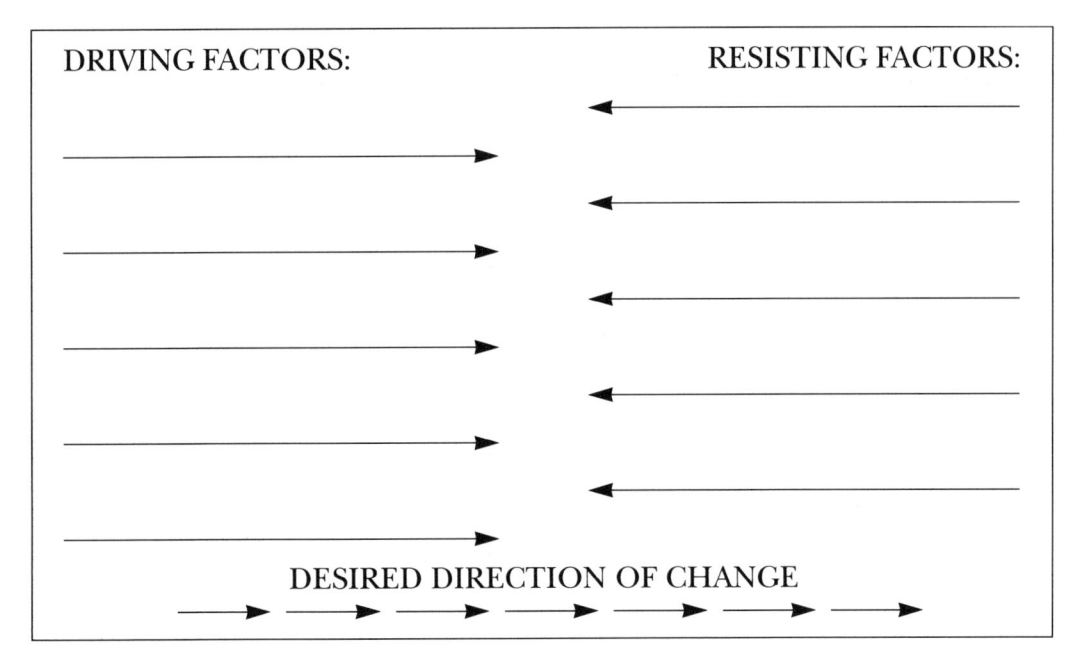

| DRIVING FACTORS: | RESISTING FACTORS: |
|---|---|
| →         →         →         →         →         → | ←         ←         ←         ←         ← |

DESIRED DIRECTION OF CHANGE
→ → → → → → →

**Adapted from Lewin's forcefield analysis model***

---

*Lewin, K, 'Group decision and social change', in T.M. Newcombe and E.L. Hartley (eds), *Readings in Social Psychology*, Holt, Rinehart and Winston, New York, 1947.

*Document 22.2 (Page 1 of 2)*

# Driving/resisting factors

1. What am I aiming to achieve?

2. What will I settle for at this stage?

3. What are the driving and resisting forces? List them in the box below.

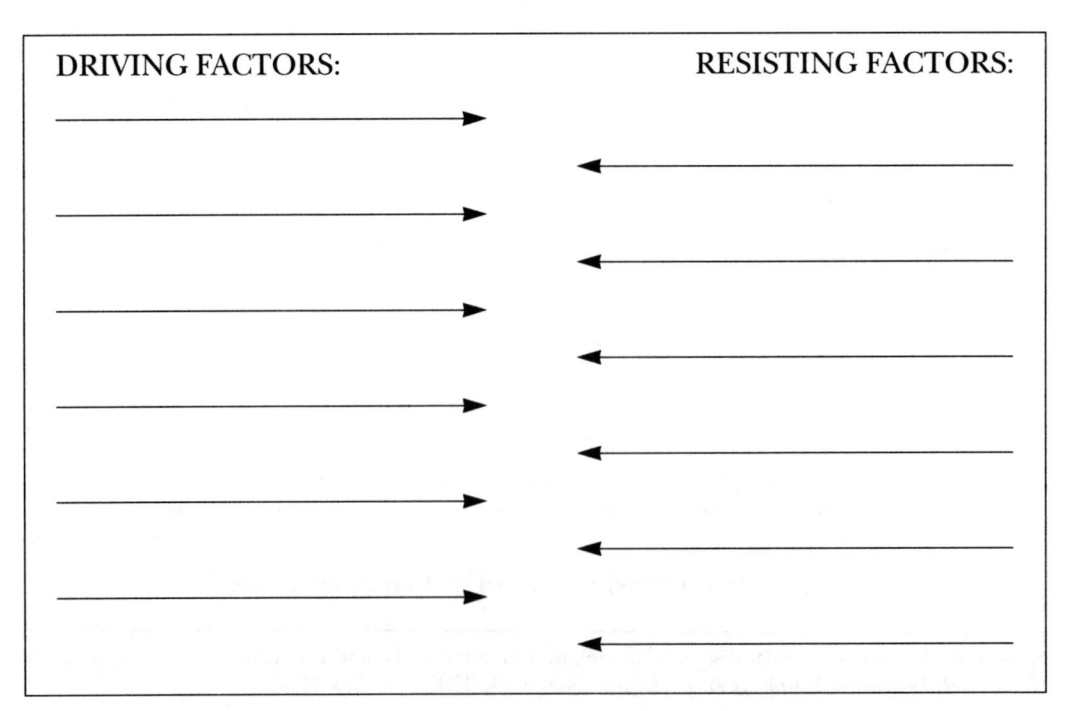

| DRIVING FACTORS: | RESISTING FACTORS: |
| --- | --- |

*Reproduced from Facilitating Change: Ready-to-use training materials for the manager by Barry Fletcher, Gower, Aldershot*

*Document 22.2 (Page 2 of 2)*

4. How can I increase my driving factors and decrease my resisting factors? What effect will these changes have on the situation?

5. How and when can I make these changes?

6. What help do I need and who can I ask?

Reproduced from *Facilitating Change: Ready-to-use training materials for the manager* by Barry Fletcher, Gower, Aldershot

*Document 22.3 (Page 1 of 1)*

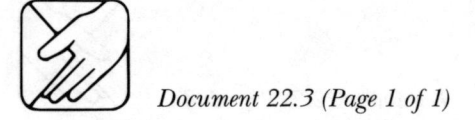

# Choices framework

| BE PERSISTENT/STOP COMPLAINING<br><br>– Can I really do this?<br>– What will it cost me?<br>– What will I need to do? etc. | WORK FOR CHANGE IN OTHERS AND/OR WORK FOR CHANGE IN THE SYSTEM<br><br>– Who/what do I want to change?<br>– How can I do this?<br>– What help do I need? etc. |
|---|---|
| GET OUT<br><br>– Where to?<br>– When?<br>– Why? etc. | WORK FOR CHANGE IN SELF<br><br>– What do I need to change in myself?<br>– How can I do this?<br>– What help do I need? etc. |

Reproduced from *Facilitating Change: Ready-to-use training materials for the manager*
by Barry Fletcher, Gower, Aldershot

*Document 22.4 (Page 1 of 2)*

# Action plan

1. What choice(s) have I decided on?

2. What do I need to do to implement my choice(s):

    (a) During next week?

    (b) During the next two to four weeks?

    (c) During the next two to three months?

Reproduced from *Facilitating Change: Ready-to-use training materials for the manager*
by Barry Fletcher, Gower, Aldershot

*Document 22.4 (Page 2 of 2)*

3. Who do I need to help me to implement my choice(s):

   (a) During next week?

   (b) During the next two to four weeks?

   (c) During the next two to three months and beyond?

4. How will I know that I am making progress?

5. What will I do if I am not progressing?

# Positive/negative self-talk

*All of us, consciously or unconsciously, talk to ourselves.*
*We talk ourselves in and out of situations every day.*
*The things we tell ourselves significantly affect the way we feel.*

You can adjust your attitude to change by altering your self-talk language. 'Yes, but ...?' displays your resistance to change. Replacing 'but' with 'and' or 'however' allows you to be more flexible and accepting of situations, more positive, less negative. Using the word 'opportunity', rather than seeing change as a 'threat', helps to remove your negative thoughts and see the diversity and power of positive thinking.

Changing your self-talk is not easy and requires conscious, continued practice before it becomes a natural part of your thought processes. Some techniques which could help speed up the process are:

(a) Look for the positive, good aspects of every experience you have. The laws of nature tell us that every negative has a positive so, if you look for it, every bad experience will have a good side to it.

(b) Avoid being negative: try instead to be more positive by using words from the right-hand column rather than the left:

| | |
|---|---|
| but | and |
| problem | opportunity |
| I must | I choose to |
| I have to | I want to |
| I can't | I can try to |
| threat | opening |
| impossible | challenging |

(c) Ask for other people's perspective on a situation – sometimes you are too close to something and this prevents you from seeing all the aspects or possibilities.

(d) Try to 'look in' on the situation from the outside, that is, be a 'fly on the wall'. Look down and watch the action, hear the dialogue and see the process as a stranger and not as an integral part of the event. Again, this can help you achieve a clear, different view of the situation.

# 23

# Discovering key organizational goals

Despite being busy in our work, we are sometimes left questioning the value of our contribution to the organization. As our understanding of what our organization is aiming to achieve increases we can start to take more informed choices about our work priorities; we can begin to make connections between our work and the organization's work; we can recognize our worth; we can become confident that we are truly 'on board'.

This group activity is designed to help participants seek out, discuss and confirm their organization's key goals.

## Benefits

Participants undertaking this activity can expect to:

- increase their knowledge and understanding of what the organization is aiming to achieve;
- check out their understanding with a senior manager who is involved in determining the strategy of the organization;
- draw their own conclusions about the organization's goals;
- plan how to close any gaps in their knowledge of organizational goals.

## Suitable for

This activity is for anyone who is interested in increasing their understanding of the organizational context within which they work. Used within a team this activity will help members to understand the connection

*Facilitating Change*

between team goals and organization goals, thus confirming the value of the team's contribution.

## What to do

As part of your preparation spend time with a senior manager or director who is involved in the process of formulating corporate objectives. Discuss your objectives in presenting the activity and invite them to the session. They need to be prepared to listen to participants' finding and conclusions and also to contribute their own knowledge and understanding of the organization's purpose, goals and objectives. They can add value to the session by describing factors and constraints which shape and inform organizational goals.

While this activity can be used on its own, there will be additional benefits from using it as the first of a group of three activities, summarized in Document 23.1, Connections between Activities 23, 24 and 3.

Should all three activities be undertaken, the findings can be recorded on Document 23.3, 'T-matrix', included as an optional exercise within this activity. The completed 'T-matrix' shows relationships between organizational, team and personal (career) goals and helps to highlight strengths, gaps or weaknesses.

1. Distribute Document 23.2 to participants, preferably two or three weeks in advance of the planned session, with a request that they complete it before they attend the session. Flexible methods can be used to find answers to the questions and may include investigation by 'digging' and asking around, together with personal opinion based on prior knowledge and experience.

2. After a brief introduction, divide participants into groups of three to five. Ask the groups to share and discuss their responses to Document 23.2 and to agree a means of feeding back a summary of their findings to the main group and the guest director or senior manager.

3. Bring participants together for each group's presentation and encourage questions from participants and your guest. Invite your guest to comment on the quality and content of participants' findings and to describe current goals of the organization and the process by which these are set.

4. End the activity with a plenary session, including the following:

    - Ask participants to share the conclusions they have formed about the organization's goals and the process for arriving at these.
    - Aim to identify any gaps in knowledge or understanding of

organizational goals perceived by participants. Discuss and agree how these gaps can be addressed, enlisting the support of the guest speaker if possible.

5. (optional) If all three activities 23, 24 and 3 are to be undertaken:

- Distribute a copy of Document 23.3, 'T-matrix', to each participant and describe its use.

- Allow time for participants to list *actual* key organizational goals in the relevant section of the matrix; that is, a1, a2, a3, etc.

- Suggest that they save the 'T-matrix' for use in the follow-on activities, 24 and 3.

## Time required

1. Completing Document 23.2 before the session takes one to two hours.

2. Sharing responses to Document 23.2 takes thirty to forty minutes.

3. The presentations and guest's contribution take sixty to ninety minutes (allowing for two groups).

4. The plenary session takes twenty to thirty minutes.

5. (optional) Completing Document 23.3, Section a, takes ten to fifteen minutes.

Average total time: two hours thirty minutes.

## Resources and materials needed

1. Sufficient copies of Documents 23.2 and 23.3 (optional).

2. Sufficient space for groups to work undisturbed.

3. Flipchart, paper and pens.

*Document 23.1 (Page 1 of 1)*

# Connections between Activities 23, 24 and 3

| **Activity 23:** Discovering key organizational goals | **Activity 24:** Developing team goals | **Activity 3:** Reordering my personal goals |
|---|---|---|
| **Organizational** *Purpose:*<br>● Why the organization was formed<br>● Why it exists now | **Team** *Purpose:*<br>● Why the team was formed<br>● Why it exists now | **Personal** *Purpose:*<br>● Aspirations<br>● Values<br>● Beliefs |
| *Ethos:* How the organization interacts with its environment, its employees and other 'stakeholders'. | *Team vision:* How the team visualizes itself within the framework of the organization. | *Personal vision:* How individuals perceive themselves within the context of their lives, their team and the organization. |
| *Organizational goals:* Objectives which relate to financial, market, growth, sales and technological factors. | *Team goals:* Objectives which reflect organizational goals and team members' aspirations. | *Personal goals:* Setting and achieving goals which embrace self, family, job and career. |
| Encourages participants to discover key organizational goals, enables them to discuss their findings in groups, and provides an opportunity to present to a senior manager for comment/ confirmation. | Encourages team members to discuss and establish team purpose and role within the organization and to clarify and agree team goals. | Encourages individuals to strive for the achievement of personal goals and to discuss these with colleagues and their manager. |

Reproduced from *Facilitating Change: Ready-to-use training materials for the manager* by Barry Fletcher, Gower, Aldershot

Document 23.2 (Page 1 of 2)

# Discovering 'key' organizational goals – questionnaire

Please complete this questionnaire in advance of the session.

This may be new territory for you, in which case you will need to search for answers. One approach may be for you to pencil in what you think are some appropriate answers based on your prior knowledge and experience. These can form the basis of a discussion with directors or senior managers.

Before you start you may wish to note the following definitions of terms used:

| | |
|---|---|
| *Purpose:* | The reason for an organization's existence. It may be considered in two respects:<br><br>(a) Why was the organization formed?<br><br>and (b) Why does it exist now? |
| *Ethos:* | This describes the behaviour of the organization towards its employees, customers, suppliers, local community, competitors and other external contacts. |
| *Goals:* | An end to be achieved, for example 'We aim to increase our share of the European market by 25 per cent over the next three years'. |

1. What is the purpose of your organization?

    (a) Why was it formed?

    (b) Why does it exist now?

Reproduced from *Facilitating Change: Ready-to-use training materials for the manager* by Barry Fletcher, Gower, Aldershot

*Document 23.2 (Page 2 of 2)*

2. How does your organization behave towards its employees and others with whom it has contact? (That is, what is its ethos towards internal and external contacts – customers, suppliers, outside establishments, etc.?)

3. Having stated the purpose and ethos of your organization, what would you say are its *key* goals? Summarize any objectives which relate to financial, sales, human resource, growth, market and technological factors.

4. What, if any, were the main difficulties you encountered in finding answers to the above questions?

Reproduced from *Facilitating Change: Ready-to-use training materials for the manager* by Barry Fletcher, Gower, Aldershot

*Document 23.3 (Page 1 of 1)*

# 'T-matrix'

The 'T-matrix' aims to show the relationship, or correlation, that exists between three separate items – in this case organizational, team and personal job or career goals. It should be completed, as follows:

1. List your organization's key goals under a1, a2, a3, ... a12.

2. List your team's key goals under c1, c2, c3, ... c12.

3. List your own (personal) career or job-related goals under b1, b2, b3, ... b12.

4. Mark on the matrix the relationship or correlation you think exists between the goals listed using the following codes: ⊙ strong correlation; ○ some correlation; ▲ possible correlation.

|  |  | a1 | a2 | a3 | a4 | a5 | a6 | a7 | a8 | a9 | a10 | a11 | a12 |
|---|---|---|---|---|---|---|---|---|---|---|---|---|---|
|  | b1 |  |  |  |  |  |  |  |  |  |  |  |  |
|  | b2 |  |  |  |  |  |  |  |  |  |  |  |  |
|  | b3 |  |  |  |  |  |  |  |  |  |  |  |  |
|  | b4 |  |  |  |  |  |  |  |  |  |  |  |  |
|  | b5 |  |  |  |  |  |  |  |  |  |  |  |  |
|  | b6 |  |  |  |  |  |  |  |  |  |  |  |  |
|  | b7 |  |  |  |  |  |  |  |  |  |  |  |  |
|  | b8 |  |  |  |  |  |  |  |  |  |  |  |  |
|  | b9 |  |  |  |  |  |  |  |  |  |  |  |  |
|  | b10 |  |  |  |  |  |  |  |  |  |  |  |  |
|  | b11 |  |  |  |  |  |  |  |  |  |  |  |  |
|  | b12 |  |  |  |  |  |  |  |  |  |  |  |  |
| Personal / Goals / Organizational / Team | | a1 | a2 | a3 | a4 | a5 | a6 | a7 | a8 | a9 | a10 | a11 | a12 |
|  | c1 |  |  |  |  |  |  |  |  |  |  |  |  |
|  | c2 |  |  |  |  |  |  |  |  |  |  |  |  |
|  | c3 |  |  |  |  |  |  |  |  |  |  |  |  |
|  | c4 |  |  |  |  |  |  |  |  |  |  |  |  |
|  | c5 |  |  |  |  |  |  |  |  |  |  |  |  |
|  | c6 |  |  |  |  |  |  |  |  |  |  |  |  |
|  | c7 |  |  |  |  |  |  |  |  |  |  |  |  |
|  | c8 |  |  |  |  |  |  |  |  |  |  |  |  |
|  | c9 |  |  |  |  |  |  |  |  |  |  |  |  |
|  | c10 |  |  |  |  |  |  |  |  |  |  |  |  |
|  | c11 |  |  |  |  |  |  |  |  |  |  |  |  |
|  | c12 |  |  |  |  |  |  |  |  |  |  |  |  |

Reproduced from *Facilitating Change: Ready-to-use training materials for the manager* by Barry Fletcher, Gower, Aldershot

# 24

# Developing team goals

This team activity is designed to help team members jointly develop realistic goals which positively contribute to organizational goals and objectives.

## Benefits

Participants undertaking this activity can expect to:

- confirm the purpose and key goals of the organization;
- develop a positive appreciation of the role of their team in the organization;
- develop team goals and objectives which positively contribute to the aims of the organization and thereby enhance their team's standing within the organization;
- anticipate likely constraints on achieving team goals;
- evaluate the team's capability for achieving agreed goals.

## Suitable for

This activity will be valuable for teams which are newly formed or have been reorganized or where members are displaying signs of confusion about team purpose. It is also applicable to established teams where confirmation or affirmation of team purpose is seen to be desirable.

The activity will interest team leaders and managers who wish to focus their team members' energies onto mutually agreed aims.

*Facilitating Change*

## What to do

As team leader you may decide to present the activity yourself or in conjunction with a colleague or experienced trainer. Co-presenting will allow you more time to concentrate with your team on the specific content of the activity. However, some pre-planning will be necessary to clarify each other's role and your plan for working together.

While this activity can be used on its own, there will be additional benefits from using it as one of a group of three interrelated activities, summarized in Document 23.1, Connections between Activities 23, 24 and 3.

Should all three activities be undertaken, the findings can be recorded on Document 23.3, 'T-matrix', included as an optional exercise within the previous activity. The completed 'T-matrix' shows relationships between organizational, team and personal goals and helps to highlight strengths, gaps or weaknesses.

Before the activity you should prepare yourself to provide information and answer questions on organizational purpose, ethos and goals, as covered by Activity 23, and current plans, policies or constraints which affect your team.

1. Distribute Document 24.1, Developing team goals – questionnaire, for participants to complete either individually or in pairs.

2. Invite the whole team to share and discuss their questionnaire responses. Their target is to reach agreement and to enter the team response onto one questionnaire. This agreed response is then presented to you as team leader.

3. As team leader you should now discuss the 'gap', if any exists, between your perceptions of the goals you believe your team should be pursuing and the perceptions of your team. The main purpose of this part of the process is to share openly any differences in perceptions, to discuss these and to work towards their reduction or removal. Aim to reach full agreement on the team's key goals.

4. After agreement has been reached invite the team to complete Document 24.2, Team goals. Your full participation at this stage is recommended.

5. End the session with an open discussion on participants' thoughts and feelings about the exercise. Ask participants to share any learning which they have gained from the activity.

6. (optional) If all three activities 23, 24 and 3 are being undertaken:

    - Allow time for participants to list *agreed* team goals in the relevant section of the 'T-matrix', that is c1, c2, c3, etc.

*Developing team goals*

- Suggest that they save the 'T-matrix' for use in Activities 23 and 3.

## Time required

1. Completing Document 24.1 takes thirty minutes.
2. Producing an agreed response to Document 24.1 takes fifty to sixty minutes.
3. Sharing differences and reaching agreement on their reduction or removal takes thirty to forty-five minutes.
4. Completing Document 24.2 takes thirty to forty-five minutes.
5. Plenary session takes fifteen minutes.
6. (optional) Completing Document 23.3, Section c, takes ten to fifteen minutes.

Average total time: three hours.

## Resources and materials needed

1. Sufficient copies of Documents 24.1 and 24.2.
2. Sufficient space for participants to work undisturbed.
3. Flipchart, paper and pens.
4. Video camera and playback facilities (optional).

*Document 24.1 (Page 1 of 2)*

# Developing team goals – questionnaire

1. *Organizational purpose and goals:*

    (a)  What is the purpose of your organization?

    (b)  What are its *key* goals?

    (*Note:* For those who have already completed Activity 23, this question will have been addressed at that time.)

2. *Team purpose:*

    (a)  What is the purpose of your team?

    (b)  Why was it formed and why does it exist now?

*Document 24.1 (Page 2 of 2)*

3. *Team vision:*

    How do you envisage your team contributing to the goals of your organization?

4. *Team goals:*

    Considering your responses to questions 1, 2 and 3, what do you consider to be your team's *key* goals?

5. Describe any problems or difficulties you experienced in developing team goals.

Reproduced from *Facilitating Change: Ready-to-use training materials for the manager* by Barry Fletcher, Gower, Aldershot

*Document 24.2 (Page 1 of 2)*

# Team goals – notes on completing form

1. List all your team's key goals in statement form. To be complete, each goal should be clear, concise and quantified, with a target time (where possible). For example, reduce the absentee rate to less than one per cent within the next six months.

2. List all the likely constraints which will hinder your team in its efforts towards achieving the goals. For example, lack of suitable equipment, poor cooperation from other departments.

3. List all the factors considered to be vital to success. For example, good communication within the team and across team interfaces, involvement of customers.

4. List all the skills required within the team for effective goal achievement. For example, fluency in 'business' French, report and letter writing, presentation skills.

5. Indicate the team's current capability in that skill: Adequate = (✔); Weak = T (training required).

6. If training is required, indicate the priority of this: Urgently = A; Within 3 months = B; Within 12 months = C.

7. Agree review dates when the team will meet to discuss goal achievement, progress, revision of goals and setting new goals.

*Document 24.2 (Page 2 of 2)*

# Team goals

| Team goals (statement) | Constraints | Factors critical to success | Skills required within the team | Capability | Priority class (A-B-C) |
|---|---|---|---|---|---|
|  |  |  |  |  |  |
| Review Dates | 1st | 2nd | 3rd | 4th | Our capability<br>Adequate ………(✔)<br>Training required ……(T) | Training is required:<br>A - Urgently<br>B - within 3 months<br>C - within 12 months |
|  |  |  |  |  |  |  |

Reproduced from *Facilitating Change: Ready-to-use training materials for the manager* by Barry Fletcher, Gower, Aldershot

# 25

# Introducing change at work

*'Innovatory approaches come only from a high degree of confidence that every thought and proposal **will make a difference:** at very least that it will become part of the **cauldron of ideas** and therefore will give other people chance to think about it and find out about it and use it to develop their own views. Thus every contribution is valuable.'*
(Paul O'Mahony, Chester, 1995)

This activity takes a proactive view of innovation in the workplace. Emphasis is given to the need for everyone to contribute to their organization's success, not just through their normal routine work but also in the generation of innovative ideas.

## Benefits

Participants undertaking this activity can expect to:

- realize that introducing change is a 'bottom-up' as well as a 'top-down' process;
- accept that they have a responsibility for innovation at work;
- see that everyone can greatly influence change;
- decide on at least two changes in their workplace and make a commitment to making these changes.

## Suitable for

This activity is suitable for all levels of employee.

*Facilitating Change*

## What to do

You will be aware of the perceptions which your staff have about their own degree of influence in bringing about change. Much depends on the culture within which they are used to working: for example, in some organizations any suggestions for change are frowned on and not welcomed, while in others suggestions may be welcomed but not acted on.

You will need to encourage people who think they have little influence to voice their discontent and to experiment with some small steps for achieving change. You may be helping others to develop strategies and skills aimed at influencing significant changes in their workplace.

In all cases, you need to concentrate on unlocking and widening participants' views on their capacity to influence change.

1. Give a brief introduction and encourage participants to share their ideas of the meaning of the word 'innovate'. Divide participants into groups of three or four and ask them to consider the following questions which should be written up on a flipchart:

    - Who usually innovates in this organization?
    - Who usually innovates in your department or section?
    - How do they do it?
    - How could we, as individuals, effect changes at work?

    Ask each group to decide on a means of feeding back their findings.

2. Bring participants together and ask groups to present their findings, allowing fifteen minutes for each group. Discuss the results, concentrating particularly on ideas for individual influence, and record the main points on a flipchart.

3. Distribute Document 25.1, Introducing change in the workplace, and ask each participant to complete it. They should work either:

    - individually,
    - by sharing ideas in pairs, or
    - by open discussion in groups.

4. Back in the main group, ask participants to share their intentions with particular attention to:

    - feasibility
    - commitment

*Introducing change at work*

- monitoring
- support and assistance from others.

Finally, invite each participant to make a commitment to two changes. Encourage discussion on these and particularly on the help that team members can give to each other in making the changes.

## Time required

1. Introduction and considering questions takes twenty-five to thirty minutes.
2. Presentations take thirty to fifty minutes.
3. Completing Document 25.1 takes thirty to forty minutes.
4. Commitment and discussion take twenty to thirty minutes.

Average total time: two hours and fifteen minutes.

## Resources and materials needed

1. Sufficient copies of Document 25.1.
2. Sufficient space for groups to work undisturbed.
3. Flipchart, paper and pens.

*Document 25.1 (Page 1 of 2)*

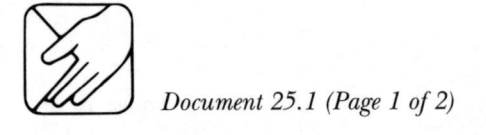

# Introducing change in the workplace

Imagine you have the power to change completely your workplace for the better – either directly or by exerting influence on others. What parts would you change?

In the last column indicate the degree of control as follows: D = in my direct control; I = cannot control but can influence; X = can neither control nor influence.

| The change you would make | Workplace changes ||||| 
|---|---|---|---|---|---|
| | Would you like to see (✔) ||| S = short term<br>L = long term<br><br>How soon? | Degree of control |
| | More of this | Less of this | This main-tained | | |
| | | | | | |

Reproduced from *Facilitating Change: Ready-to-use training materials for the manager*
by Barry Fletcher, Gower, Aldershot

Document 25.1 (Page 2 of 2)

Choose *two* of the listed changes, one you can 'directly' control and one you can 'influence' and preferably the ones you would like to see implemented quickly. Then complete the 'change plans' below:

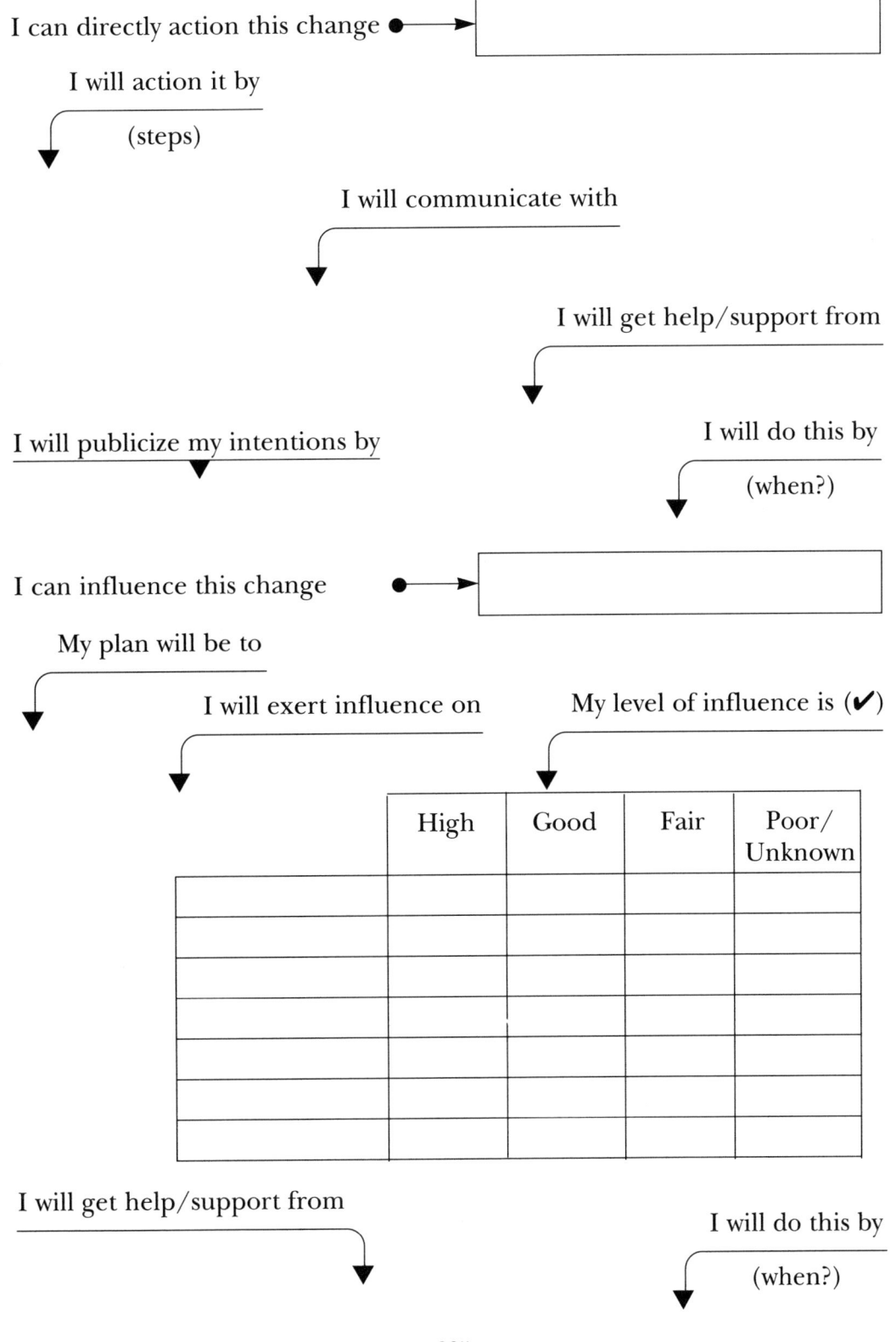

I can directly action this change ●⟶ ☐

    I will action it by
    ⎯⎯⎯⎯⎯⎯⎯⎯⎯⎯⎯⎯⎯
        (steps)
▼

            I will communicate with
            ⎯⎯⎯⎯⎯⎯⎯⎯⎯⎯⎯⎯⎯⎯⎯⎯
            ▼

                        I will get help/support from
                        ⎯⎯⎯⎯⎯⎯⎯⎯⎯⎯⎯⎯⎯⎯⎯⎯⎯⎯
                        ▼

I will publicize my intentions by        I will do this by
⎯⎯⎯⎯⎯⎯⎯⎯⎯⎯⎯⎯⎯⎯⎯⎯⎯⎯        ⎯⎯⎯⎯⎯⎯⎯⎯⎯⎯
▼                                                  (when?)
                                                    ▼

I can influence this change    ●⟶ ☐

   My plan will be to
   ⎯⎯⎯⎯⎯⎯⎯⎯⎯⎯⎯
▼

            I will exert influence on        My level of influence is (✔)
            ⎯⎯⎯⎯⎯⎯⎯⎯⎯⎯⎯⎯⎯⎯⎯⎯⎯       ⎯⎯⎯⎯⎯⎯⎯⎯⎯⎯⎯⎯⎯⎯⎯⎯⎯
            ▼                                              ▼

|  | High | Good | Fair | Poor/Unknown |
|---|---|---|---|---|
|  |  |  |  |  |
|  |  |  |  |  |
|  |  |  |  |  |
|  |  |  |  |  |
|  |  |  |  |  |
|  |  |  |  |  |
|  |  |  |  |  |

I will get help/support from                            I will do this by
⎯⎯⎯⎯⎯⎯⎯⎯⎯⎯⎯⎯⎯⎯⎯⎯⎯⎯⎯⎯            ⎯⎯⎯⎯⎯⎯⎯⎯⎯⎯
                              ▼                                       (when?)
                                                                                         ▼

Reproduced from *Facilitating Change: Ready-to-use training materials for the manager* by Barry Fletcher, Gower, Aldershot

# 26

# Striving for internal quality

*'If we cannot provide excellent quality of service to ourselves inside the organization, then how can we delight our customers outside the organization?'*

This group activity enables participants to review their attitudes towards internal quality and offers a framework for personal improvement and change. By the end of the activity the important part which everyone plays in a number of 'supplier–customer' chains will have been highlighted.

## Benefits

Participants undertaking this activity can expect to:

- gain increased awareness of their individual and group standards of quality;
- identify the quality of service they are providing to their internal customers;
- identify the quality of service they are receiving from their internal suppliers;
- generate an action plan for improving internal quality of service.

## Suitable for

This activity is suitable for any group of people in the organization who provide service to, and receive service from, each other. Used within a team

*Facilitating Change*

the activity will highlight the interdependence between team members and the relationships with others outside the team.

## What to do

Most people can recognize aspects of good quality of a product or service and all too frequently have vivid memories of the opposite. This activity encourages participants to describe some of their experiences of good and bad quality as seen through their own eyes as customers. Detailed examination of these experiences promotes understanding of the ingredients of satisfaction or dissatisfaction.

You should help participants to recognize the considerable influence they have in shaping numerous 'quality chains' within the organization. Part of the process is to broaden their perception of quality and the many ways they affect it, through their actions or non-actions, as customers or as suppliers.

Evaluation of each person's contribution to internal quality, and also the contribution made by their suppliers, will move each participant towards producing an action plan for improving the inputs they receive and the outputs they provide.

1. Distribute Document 26.1, Product/service quality evaluation form, and ask participants to complete it individually, allowing about twenty minutes. This involves describing an incident they have experienced which illustrates bad quality of product or service.

2. Divide participants into small groups of three or four and ask them to share and discuss their chosen incident with each other. Ask each group to complete a flipchart sheet showing their consolidated view of 'components of quality'.

3. Back in the main group ask each group to announce its findings by giving short presentations or maybe by a 'collage' of the flipcharts for everyone to see and discuss. The group will gain from being encouraged to explore both common ground and differences.

4. In the main group set a task to identify participants' definitions of quality. This could be by brainstorming, using a whiteboard and asking participants to enter their own definitions, or by one person writing definitions on to a flipchart, etc.

   Next, ask participants to discuss the range of definitions. Thought-provoking questions could be:

   - Why are there so many variations?
   - What single definition can we all agree on?

- Where do suppliers and customers fit into these definitions?

5. Distribute Document 26.2, Internal quality – evaluation form, to each participant and divide the group into pairs. Brief each pair to work together, each partner helping the other to work through the document and to develop a clear action plan designed to improve the quality of their outputs and inputs.

6. Back in the main group ask participants to share their action plans with the group, placing particular emphasis on who can help in achieving their plans. If this activity is carried out with participants from the same department or team there is every likelihood that some 'supplier–customer' chains will exist within the group. This fact can be worked with in gaining commitments to the implementation of action plans.

    Finally, ask the group to reflect on the process of the activity and to share some of the learning gained from taking part in it.

## Time required

1. Completing Document 26.1 takes twenty minutes.
2. Sharing and producing consolidated views take twenty to thirty minutes.
3. Discussing components of quality takes twenty minutes.
4. Identifying definitions of quality takes twenty to thirty minutes.
5. Completing Document 26.2 and action plans takes sixty to ninety minutes.
6. Sharing action plans and reviewing take twenty to thirty minutes.

Average total time: half a day, including breaks.

## Resources and materials needed

1. Sufficient copies of Documents 26.1 and 26.2.
2. Sufficient space for participants to work undisturbed.
3. Flipchart, paper and pens.

*Document 26.1 (Page 1 of 2)*

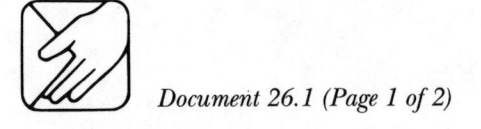

# Product/service quality evaluation form

How do you react when you are given a poor-quality product or service? What is the point at which you will complain if things are not right? For many people the point at which they will complain often depends on the circumstances and the values or costs involved.

Complete the chart below by placing an 'X' on the satisfaction scale to indicate the points at which you would complain in each of the given situations:

| Situation | Satisfaction scale<br>0  1  2  3   4  5   6  7  8   9  10<br>Extremely dissatisfied   Less<br>and frustrated/angry   than        Satisfied         Highly<br>with outcome         satisfied                      satisfied |
|---|---|
| *High-value product/service*<br>For example, new car, interior design of house | |
| *Medium-value product/service*<br>For example, new camera, package holiday | |
| *Low-value product/service*<br>For example, ballpoint pen, shoe repair | |

Now describe an incident where you received a poor-quality product or service:

What went wrong?

240

Reproduced from *Facilitating Change: Ready-to-use training materials for the manager* by Barry Fletcher, Gower, Aldershot

*Document 26.1 (Page 2 of 2)*

What did you do about the incident?

Next, using the table below, list in the left-hand column the ingredients which make up a good-quality product or service:

| Good-quality product or service ||
|---|---|
| Component (ingredient) | Satisfaction rating<br>0 1 2 3 4 5 6 7 8 9 10<br>Low                       High |
|  |  |

Rate the incident you have described against each ingredient you have identified.

If the same situation happened again, how would you handle it?

Document 26.2 (Page 1 of 2)

# Internal quality – evaluation form: instructions

1. List your internal customers (those people in the organization who rely on you for any product or service).

2. List your 'outputs' to your internal customers: what you provide them with.

3. For each of your internal customers make an estimate of the quality level you believe you are currently achieving for them against each of the listed outputs. Use a scale of 1 (low) to 10 (high).
   *Note:* Obviously you will need to be honest with yourself here and since this form is for your private use there is no excuse not to be. Consider, when scoring, any work you know that you passed which you felt at the time fell below your own usual good standards. Also, think about any complaints or poor feedback you may have had recently – was it justified?

4. Circle any score numbers which fall *below* your own minimum standards of quality, that is, the standard at which you would complain if you were the receiver.

5. Repeat Steps 1 to 4 for your internal suppliers (those people within the organization on whom you rely for a product or service).

6. Using your completed sheet as a guide, produce an action plan for improving internal quality. This may need to address the following types of problem:

   (a) Significant variation, or lower than acceptable levels in *output* quality, may indicate a need for you to give more care and attention to some, if not all, internal customers. This could involve encouraging customers to be more specific about their needs and requirements, speaking to them and using skilful questions combined with good listening. This equates to you working more skilfully as a 'supplier'.

   (b) Significant variation, or lower than acceptable levels in *input* quality from your suppliers, may indicate a need for you to consult more closely with them. Spend more time defining your needs and expectations clearly. This equates to you being more skilful as a 'customer'.

Reproduced from *Facilitating Change: Ready-to-use training materials for the manager* by Barry Fletcher, Gower, Aldershot

# Internal quality – evaluation form

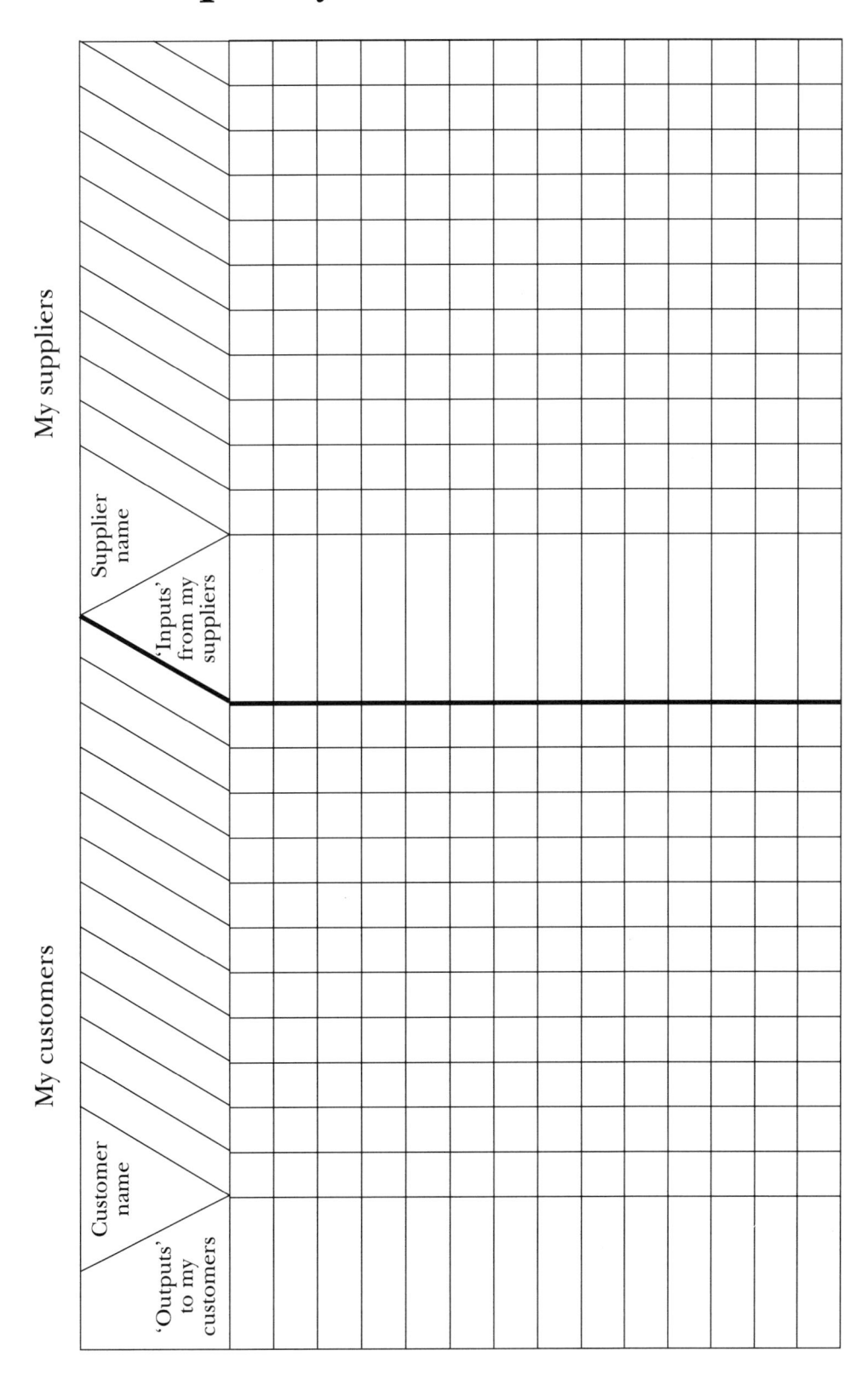

*My suppliers*

Supplier name

'Inputs' from my suppliers

*My customers*

Customer name

'Outputs' to my customers

# 27

# Introducing new patterns of work

*'So you take every opportunity to grab the imagination of your employees, you get them to feel they are doing something important, that they are not a lone voice, that they are the most powerful and potent people on the planet'*
(Anita Roddick, *Body and Soul*, Ebury Press, 1991)

This dynamic, creative, group activity is particularly suited to organizations which accept that all staff have views, opinions and suggestions which can lead to improvement. The activity encourages participants to question present arrangements for work organization; it also provides a platform for participants to think creatively about the type of changes in working patterns which they believe would lead to improvements.

This activity can be approached from two different levels – the total organization or the department, section or team – and you may wish to incorporate one or both of these when using the activity.

## Benefits

Participants undertaking this activity can expect to:

- assess critically their current work patterns;
- generate a list of alternative ways of working;
- identify viable alternative work patterns and produce an action plan for implementing change within their immediate work area; and/or
- present a case for changing work patterns to senior management and receive feedback together with agreement on next steps.

*Facilitating Change*

## Suitable for

The reasons for undertaking the activity could be numerous. For example, a team or department may be performing well but at the same time recognizes the need to examine critically its ways of working in order to continue to perform well in the future; a section may not be performing well and seeks to rearrange its working patterns; an organization may wish to generate employees' ideas and suggestions on work patterns as an input to forward business planning.

## What to do

You need to create an atmosphere of openness and trust when inviting participants to make a critical appraisal of current work patterns and to suggest changes. The quality of data generated will depend on this supportive atmosphere. You will need to 'pave the way' by reducing apprehensions and fear of recrimination, thus enabling participants to feel comfortable when sharing their thoughts and feelings about the present order of things.

The process involves close examination of the way we do things now, even if it is currently successful, moving on to how might we do things differently and what would be the benefits of changing. Your role is to work towards a climate where such discussion can take place, dealing with destructive and negative behaviours and encouraging participants to think creatively about alternative ways of working.

Where the activity concerns organizational issues, you can help by setting up appropriate support and arranging for participants' suggestions to be heard by senior people in the organization who can influence policy. You could arrange for these people to attend at the appropriate time; brief them to listen carefully to presentations; encourage them to ask questions; explain to them the importance of treating suggestions positively and being prepared to incorporate this valuable data in their decision-making processes.

1. Introduce the activity, emphasizing the value of candid comments and creative thinking throughout the process. As a warm-up exercise ask participants to brainstorm the theme of patterns of work. This process should produce different perceptions of the theme and help to provide a good start to Step 2.

2. Divide participants into groups whose composition reflects common interest in the particular area to be pursued (that is, organization, department, section, team or even individual). Distribute Document 27.1, Introducing new patterns of work, to all participants. Allow some

*Introducing new patterns of work*

time for questions and clarification of the task to be undertaken and the time allowed.

3. In the main group allow time for each group to present its suggestions for new patterns of working. Participants should ask questions, and give constructive criticism and feedback. Hold a debate on the advantages of proposed changes over current patterns of working.

4. Ask participants to reform into their groups and undertake the task outlined in Document 27.2 (for the organization approach) or Document 27.3 (for the department, section or team approach).

5. Back in the main group allow time for presentations and encourage discussion and questions. Where the approach is organizational, ensure any senior executives contract clearly with the group on next steps.

6. In a plenary session discuss the activity, the sharing of thoughts on the process, and the learning which participants feel has resulted.

## Time required

1. Introduction and brainstorming take twenty minutes.
2. Completing Document 27.1 takes one hour thirty minutes to two hours.
3. Sharing suggestions and advantages of proposed changes takes thirty to forty minutes.
4. Completing Document 27.2 or 27.3 takes thirty to forty-five minutes.
5. Presentations take sixty to ninety minutes.
6. Plenary session takes twenty to thirty minutes.

Average total time: between one half and one full day, including breaks.

## Resources and materials needed

1. Sufficient copies of Documents 27.1, 27.2 and 27.3.
2. Sufficient space for participants to work undisturbed.
3. Flipcharts, paper and pens.
4. Presence of senior executive(s), suitably briefed, if addressing organizational issues.
5. Video camera and playback facilities (optional).

*Document 27.1 (Page 1 of 2)*

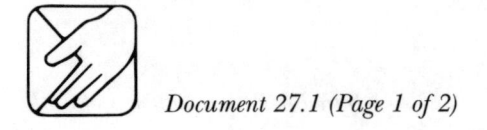

# Introducing new patterns of work

## 1. A critical look at current work patterns

This task provides an opportunity to review the ways in which work is done now in your organization or immediate area. To start your thinking you may wish to consider the following questions and add others as you progress:

- What is the purpose of our work?
- Why does the organization require our work to be done?
- How does the organization require our work to be done?
- How well is our work pattern geared to the needs of our customers (internal and external)?
- Why is our work done in the way it is?
- What forces things to be done in the way they are?
- Where and when does our work need to be done?
- What demarcation exists, and why?
- How do we behave in our work and why is this?
- How flexible are we in our work?
- How well covered are we for the unexpected?

## 2. Alternative patterns of work

Your group can now spend time identifying alternative ways of doing things. Ideas and suggestions should be allowed to flow freely – no matter how outlandish or bizarre they seem. You may wish to consider 'brainstorming' to release people's thoughts on other, different ways in which your work could be organized. Another means is to consider some key questions, such as:

- If we had complete freedom how would we organize our work?
- How would we like to do our work?
- How could our work be done differently?
- What do we believe would improve it?

You will be able to add your own questions as you proceed: the main purpose of this stage is to generate a wide range of alternatives.

## 3. Choosing viable alternatives

Produce a concise statement of any criteria which would need to be met by any new or revised pattern of working. In completing this you will need to consider factors such as meeting customer needs and expectations; effective use of your resources, time, skill and knowledge, etc.

Having agreed these criteria, determine how far each of your alternative methods of working would meet them. Refine your list of alternatives to leave only those which meet *all* criteria.

## 4. Ranking the viable alternatives

Rank your refined list in order of preference: again you may wish to agree some criteria for doing this. For example, highest perceived benefits; appeal to customers; ease of changing; degree of personal influence in making the change; attractiveness to staff, etc.

## 5. Choosing areas for change

Finally, from your ranked list, choose the alternative(s) you would be prepared to invest time and energy in pursuing further. In preparation for presenting to the main group, record your chosen alternatives on flipchart paper together with the benefits which you believe would arise from the change. You will need to be clear about the advantages of your choice(s) over current working practices.

Decide how you are going to present your choices to the main group.

Reproduced from *Facilitating Change: Ready-to-use training materials for the manager*
by Barry Fletcher, Gower, Aldershot

*Document 27.2 (Page 1 of 1)*

# Preparing a presentation (organizational approach)

Prepare a presentation on new methods of working to be made to one or more senior executives who can influence organizational policy. Include in the presentation:

- Your rationale.
- Your proposed change(s) in working patterns.
- The benefits and advantages over current practices.
- Your thoughts on resource implications.
- Your suggestions for implementation.

Reproduced from *Facilitating Change: Ready-to-use training materials for the manager* by Barry Fletcher, Gower, Aldershot

*Document 27.3 (Page 1 of 1)*

# Preparing a presentation (department/section/team approach)

Prepare a presentation, to be made to the main group, of your plan for achieving your changed working patterns. Include in the presentation:

- Specific changes to be made.
- Benefits of these changes.
- Timescale of your plan.
- Responsibilities for implementation.
- Support and monitoring arrangements.

Reproduced from *Facilitating Change: Ready-to-use training materials for the manager* by Barry Fletcher, Gower, Aldershot

# 28

# Creating customer-conscious attitudes

*'We exist, as a business, for no other reason than to delight our customers'*

This group activity aims to raise the level of awareness with regard to customers – who they are, how they should be treated and how participants can influence the promotion of customer-conscious attitudes within their organization.

## Benefits

Participants undertaking this activity can expect to:

- increase their awareness of how customers expect and deserve to be treated;
- identify how they can influence the promotion of customer-conscious attitudes within the organization;
- commit themselves to behaviour changes which will improve attitudes towards customers.

## Suitable for

This activity is suitable for anyone who is interested in developing their understanding of customer–supplier relationships. Used within a team the activity will help members to concentrate their attitude towards all the team's customers, both internally and externally.

*Facilitating Change*

## What to do

Your main role is facilitative but you can prepare by thinking about and defining the three key words: customer, conscious and attitude. Also prepare three flipchart sheets: the first with the word 'CUSTOMER' in a box in the centre, the second with the word 'CONSCIOUS' and the third with the word 'ATTITUDE'. You will need to display these sheets in a prominent position where further writing can be added to them.

1. Inform the group that as an introduction to the activity they are going to explore the expression 'customer-conscious attitude'. Invite participants to come forward and visit each sheet to write their definitions of the words around the boxes.

    Encourage a group discussion to arrive at common understanding of what is meant by the phrase 'customer-conscious attitude'.

2. Distribute Document 28.1, Holiday of a lifetime, and ask participants to spend thirty minutes reading the story and completing the exercise individually.

3. Divide participants into groups and ask them to discuss the exercise, record the main points raised and arrive at an agreed score for each character in the story.

    Back in the main group allow time for responses, encouraging questions and discussion on points raised. Ask participants to record their own key learning points.

4. Ask participants to reform into their groups and instruct them to undertake the following:

    (a) Discuss how you, individually and as a group, can influence 'customer-conscious attitudes' within this organization. Remember to consider both your 'internal' and your 'external' customers. Record your main points for future reference.

After twenty minutes introduce the next task:

    (b) Design a slogan which will raise the level of customer awareness within the organization. The slogan could be witty, humorous or in cartoon form – groups have free licence to use whatever creative means they like.

5. Ask each group to display and discuss its slogan. End with a plenary session during which each participant publicly announces at least two behaviours which they are committed to try over the next one or two weeks. These behaviours should clearly link with intended improvements

in 'customer-conscious attitudes' and participants should be prepared to challenge and question each other if such links are not apparent.

## Time required

1. Discussion and reaching common understanding take fifteen to twenty minutes.
2. Completing Document 28.1 individually takes thirty minutes.
3. Sharing and discussing group responses and recording key learning points take fifty minutes to one hour.
4. Discussion and designing slogans take thirty-five to forty-five minutes.
5. Displaying slogans and announcing intended behaviours take twenty to thirty minutes.

Average total time: three hours including a short break.

## Resources and materials needed

1. Sufficient copies of Document 28.1.
2. Sufficient space for groups to work undisturbed.
3. Flipchart, paper and pens.

Document 28.1 (Page 1 of 6)

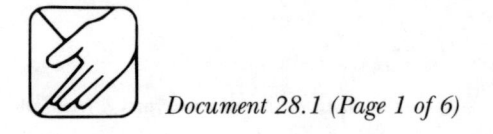

# Holiday of a lifetime

Read the following short story before completing the exercise at the end.

Tom and Kate had been looking forward to their holiday in Portugal all year; it was, after all, their first for over five years. However, there had been problems. Despite booking it almost a year in advance, the travel company had twice double-booked them, giving Tom's boss the problem of rearranging his staff holiday planner not once but twice, on the second occasion exclaiming that he was not amused and that a third change would not be tolerated.

With just three weeks to go Kate received a telephone call from the travel company booking clerk.

'Change the dates again!' shrieked Kate down the phone.

'Yes, I'm sorry Mrs Harvey, but there's been a computer error and unfortunately the fisherman's cottage has already been let to another agency and it was done before we offered it to you so we have no say in the matter,' replied the clerk, sounding as though she was eating her lunch while talking.

Kate controlled her voice and hid her anger while explaining to the booking clerk that another change was out of the question due to her husband's circumstances at work. The clerk responded as though pre-programmed, 'I'm sorry, Mrs Harvey, but there's nothing we can do. You'll have to change the dates or accept alternative accommodation, but I'll tell you now we've only got luxury apartments available at this time of year and they're about £150 per person extra per week. You'll have to let me know quickly though because I can't hold them forever.' The clerk was quite indifferent to Mrs Harvey's problems.

Within minutes Tom was listening to his wife's angry tones. He responded quickly with equal anger, now aimed at the travel company manager. 'I don't care how it's happened or who or what's to blame,' snapped Tom, 'but you'd better sort it out at your end this time because we're not changing our plans again. We've got confirmation from you in writing for a fisherman's cottage during the last two weeks in August and as far as I'm concerned that's it. Ring me back when you've sorted it!' The phone slammed down without giving the travel agency manager a chance to get a word in.

Two hours later the manager was sheepishly telling Tom about an alternative offer. A luxury villa could be provided, at no extra cost, for the last two weeks in August. The Harveys could not believe their luck as they discussed it that evening. More space, more facilities and a much improved view and all at no extra cost – all because of a 'computer error'.

\* \* \*

'Cases packed, electric off, water off, windows shut. We're just waiting for

Reproduced from *Facilitating Change: Ready-to-use training materials for the manager* by Barry Fletcher, Gower, Aldershot

Document 28.1 (Page 2 of 6)

baby now,' called Tom to his wife who was trying to coax Marie, their eight-month-old baby, to have the last ounce of milk. 'And the taxi,' replied Kate, feeling a little anxious that it was already a couple of minutes late. She had in fact booked it two weeks ago and had confirmed the details again only yesterday.

'Tom, I think you'd better phone them, he's already twenty minutes late and it's going to be tight.'

'Yes, he's leaving it a bit close, isn't he?' replied Tom, now just as anxious ...

'Ah, good morning. We've booked a taxi for eight o'clock this morning, the name's Harvey, Tom Harvey. We're a bit concerned because he's not arrived yet.' No answer – the phone was dead. Had she cut him off or was she checking? Tom waited and was just about to put the phone down to dial again when he heard the line crackle with intermittent speech as though someone was flicking between lines. Again there was a pause for what seemed ages.

'Mr Harsey? Yes, you're down for eight o'clock, West Court Terrace, OK?'

'No, no!' exclaimed Tom. He thought she was about to hang up on him. 'You see, he's already twenty minutes late and we'll be late for the coach. By the way, it's Harvey.'

'Sorry?'

'Harvey, the name's Harvey,' replied Tom, now beginning to wonder if he was trying to converse with a machine.

'Ah yes, Harvey. Well, I'm sure he'll be there soon so I wouldn't worry yourself, OK?' Tom sensed she was again about to hang up.

'Wait! Wait! Just hold it a moment. Is there any way you can contact the driver to find out just where he is?' asked Tom.

'Mr Harsey, you'll just have to be patient, our drivers can't be held to deadlines, not these days what with all the traffic and what have you ... he'll not be far away.' The line went dead again. Tom looked at his watch; the taxi was now 25 minutes late. They had just half an hour to make the coach and it was a fifteen-minute journey to the coach station. The line crackled.

'Mr Harsey, the driver's stuck in traffic, he'll be with you in five minutes. You see, I told you that's where he'd be.' The phone went dead without Tom getting a word in.

'Sorry Guv,' called the taxi driver to Tom who was rushing towards him with two large cases. 'My last fare was arguing the price. Refused to pay, he did, till I threatened him with the police. Anyway, you've got a coach to catch Guv ... don't worry, we'll have you there on time,' he offered reassuringly. The driver quickly loaded up and promptly sped off. The Harveys felt sure he was probably speeding more than perhaps he usually did. They smiled at each other, confident they would now make it.

The taxi drew up alongside the coach, its driver helping Kate and Marie out of the cab before whisking out the luggage and placing it at the feet of

Reproduced from *Facilitating Change: Ready-to-use training materials for the manager* by Barry Fletcher, Gower, Aldershot

*Document 28.1 (Page 3 of 6)*

the coach driver who by now had just about loaded up all the other passengers' luggage.

'There you are,' smiled the cabbie, 'told you I'd get you there on time. Anyway, have a good holiday and you just take care of that baby – watch she doesn't get too much sun, she's a little cracker!' Tom paid, tipped and thanked the cabbie before turning towards the coach driver.

'Will there be room?' enquired Tom, nodding towards their luggage.

'Bloody hell!' retorted the coach driver. 'There'll have to be won't there? Anybody'd think you were going for a year,' he grumbled, squeezing the cases into the back with little regard for the contents. The baby buggy was pushed into a crevice with great force and Tom was sure he heard something crack.

During the hour's drive to the airport Tom kept thinking about the buggy – wondering what, if anything, could have broken. He knew it was of sturdy construction but he was nevertheless determined to check it over before he let the driver disappear.

\* \* \*

Last in, first out – Tom was now holding up the other passengers while arguing with the driver about the buggy. The driver's clumsiness had caused the harness to snap at the buckle. The driver, however, was adamant that he had not caused the problem.

'Look, that must have been damaged before I loaded it. Anyway, I can't stand round here arguing all day. You're holding everybody up, these people have got planes to catch you know. Come on, take your bags and let me unload this lot,' muttered the driver, now starting to unload the other cases and acting as though Tom was no longer there.

Nothing more could be done now, but the Harveys were determined to complain on their return. Kate had already decided to make some makeshift repair using string once she could get hold of some. What no one had noticed, however, was that the destination ticket attached to one of their cases had also been snagged and was now only held by a thread.

Movement through passport control was smooth, but Kate and Tom agreed that they would be much happier once they were airborne.

The trainee baggage handler noticed a large blue case straddling two trolleys. On inspection he could see that it did not have a destination ticket.

'Jim! This one's got no ticket', shouted the trainee to his mentor. Jim looked up, not wanting to walk the few yards to where Ian, the trainee, was crouched over the case.

'No ticket? Are you sure?'

'Which trolley was it on then?' called Jim, still not wanting to make the short journey.

'Don't know', replied Ian, 'it was between these two. Shouldn't we open it or something?'

'No, no lad, put it on there,' pointing to the right-hand trolley.

Reproduced from *Facilitating Change: Ready-to-use training materials for the manager* by Barry Fletcher, Gower, Aldershot

'But it might ...'

'Don't argue lad, just put it on there, it'll be all right,' shouted Jim, now raising his voice slightly and adding '... on the night' quietly under his breath. Ian obeyed.

The flight was an uneventful one with baby Marie sleeping most of the time, once she had been settled by Kate and the very cheerful air hostess for whom nothing seemed too much trouble. She had quickly responded to Marie's crying by producing a set of brightly coloured plastic keys and coaxed her into taking them with all the skill of a trained nanny.

'Nice to see some professionalism at last,' whispered Tom while nodding towards the air hostess who was by now busily attending to someone else's needs.

'Yes, and she smiles too!' responded Kate.

\* \* \*

Tom looked apprehensive while staring at the now nearly empty luggage conveyor. Kate was trying unsuccessfully to feed Marie in the airport lounge. Their first case had come down the conveyor fairly quickly and they were hopeful of being through customs, away and settled in the villa within the hour.

The conveyor was empty, the second case had not appeared. Tom made his way to the information desk where a young Portuguese attendant immediately responded to his frantic appeal.

'It's a large blue case – it's full of our baby's clothes and things, we must find it, all her bottles and sterilizer are in there.'

The attendant responded well. She tried to calm Tom down and reassure him that everything would be done to find the missing case. She immediately instigated a search, while another attendant took over the desk. Despite her shared concern and thoroughness of search with double checks throughout, nothing was found. The case, baby Marie's case, had not arrived in Portugal.

Tom went through the formalities of completing the appropriate documentation. The information attendant advised Tom that he should take up the matter immediately with the tour firm's courier as there was nothing more she could do except ensure that the case, if found, was immediately delivered to their villa. She had been very kind and reassuring and really did look as despondent as Tom.

Marie was fast asleep in Kate's arms. 'I think you should phone the courier now,' suggested Kate, 'We really must have that case, it's got all Marie's things in it. I don't know how we're going to cope if we don't find it.' Tom agreed, he knew that they were not due to meet the courier until 11.00 a.m. the following morning but realized this was an emergency. The number rang continually until finally Tom gave up in despair.

They took a taxi to the villa, the tour company minibus having long gone. Its driver did not want to get involved in a 'missing luggage' problem, it was

Document 28.1 (Page 5 of 6)

not his concern. He did not even offer any words of help but shrugged his shoulders and drove off with just two passengers.

The Harveys arrived at the villa just as the Portuguese caretaker was bout to leave. She showed noticeable surprise at their arrival. In broken English she explained to them, while waving a clipboard under their noses, that she had been expecting them over two hours ago. Two young Englishmen had arrived, also from their flight, and had claimed they were booked into the villa. She was confused because she did not have their names on her list, but they showed her proof of their booking by way of the travel company documents which clearly detailed the villa, address and dates. She had waited for over an hour before finally giving way and allowing the two young men into the place, thinking it was yet 'another' error on the part of the tour company ... something that, she implied, happened occasionally.

Kate pleaded with her to allow them into the villa. The caretaker refused with much arm flapping and explained that the two Englishmen had already unpacked, gone to the town disco and would probably not be back till three, maybe four in the morning. She produced a hotel address which was apparently often used as back-up in eventualities such as this. She phoned the hotel and made arrangements for the Harveys to book into a double room. She also called a taxi, bade them farewell, and left explaining that the taxi would soon arrive. It arrived just under an hour later.

'What a breathtaking view,' thought Tom as the taxi moved away from the luxury villa he thought was theirs. Kate was near to tears as she gazed along the moonlit bay they were now leaving behind.

At 12.45 a.m. the taxi drew up to their new location – a five-storey hotel three miles inland.

The Harveys were not amused at being on the fifth floor of a dilapidated hotel with no lift, but they were too weary to argue the point that night. Besides, there was nothing that the manager could have done, they had after all taken his last double room. It was just unfortunate that it happened to be on the top floor.

\* \* \*

One hour's flying time from home, Kate was gazing pensively at the 'cotton-wool balls' below. Tom was busily drafting a list of the people he was going to write to: the tour company, ABTA, *That's Life* and even his MP, if need be. The holiday had been a shambles. The travel courier had been very elusive and had failed to resolve their accommodation problem. This was made worse by the fact that some of the money they had put aside to hire a car had to be spent on Marie's essentials that were needed to replace those in the missing case of which nothing had been heard. Without the car their treks had been limited to the three-mile journey to the coastal town by bus, the regularity of which was unpredictable.

The travel courier seemed very sympathetic at their first meeting but thereafter became very elusive and never kept any of the promises which she made. She had tried to give the impression that she was overworked and

*Document 28.1 (Page 6 of 6)*

constantly hassled by an overwhelming number of problems. After a while, Tom's queries about the missing case began to draw parrot-like responses from her such as 'Don't worry about it, if it doesn't show up you can always claim more on the insurance than the value of the contents.'

The Harveys eventually realized, after talking to fellow tourists after their brief courier meetings, that this particular courier did not seem to fulfil any of her promises, no matter how small the task. The Harveys had actually seen her around the town and on the beach looking more like a tourist than someone paid to look after their interests, a point that Tom was determined to emphasize in his letter of complaint.

'Do you think we're being paranoid writing all these letters?' asked Tom, furiously scribbling away on his pad.

'What dear?' asked Kate, suddenly jerked out of her reverie by Tom's question.

'Do you think we're being paranoid writing all these letters?'

'No! definitely not! That firm ought to be sued for the trouble they've caused us.' Kate's response caused Tom to put even more venom into his pen.

As the Harveys disembarked from the plane the air hostess smiled and said, 'Hope you enjoyed your holiday and flight.'

Kate responded. 'Thank you, it was the holiday of a lifetime!'

Judge the 'customer-conscious attitude' of each of the main characters in this story and record your verdict on a scale of 1 to 10 (1 being low, and 10 being high) in the following table. Indicate with a tick whether any 'failings' were due to acts or omissions, or both.

| The characters (in order of appearance) | Scale | Acts (tick) | Omissions (tick) |
|---|---|---|---|
| Travel company booking clerk | | | |
| Travel company manager | | | |
| Taxi company telephonist/controller | | | |
| Taxi driver | | | |
| Coach driver | | | |
| Trainee baggage handler (Ian) | | | |
| Experienced baggage handler (Jim) | | | |
| Air hostess (1st) | | | |
| Information desk attendant | | | |
| Minibus driver | | | |
| Portuguese caretaker | | | |
| Travel company courier | | | |

Reproduced from *Facilitating Change: Ready-to-use training materials for the manager* by Barry Fletcher, Gower, Aldershot

# 29

# Shifting our attitudes to service

*'I believe that service – whether it is serving the community or your family or the people you love or whatever – is fundamental to what life is about'.*
(Anita Roddick, *Body and Soul*, Ebury Press, 1991)

A challenging group activity, this takes a look at why customer service goes wrong and examines the impact of social attitudes together with 'management-controllable' failings. The activity also prompts participants to consider how they can influence the service they provide, and receive, by means of their own behaviour.

## Benefits

Participants undertaking this activity can expect to:

- identify what goes wrong when customer service fails;
- differentiate between management failings and social attitude problems;
- make individual action plans to improve the service they provide to their 'customers' and the service they receive.

## Suitable for

This activity is suitable for anyone who is interested in exploring and understanding the factors which constitute good service. Used within a team the activity will raise insights into the quality of service between team members and the service given and received by the team as a whole.

*Facilitating Change*

## What to do

Attitudes to customer service are affected by the social attitudes of the individual and the group and also by the degree of management commitment to service. This activity examines two areas: management failings and social attitudes.

Management failings cover such issues as poor selection of employees, lack of good-quality training, low morale, poor job satisfaction, inadequate supervision and weak career structures. Industrial relations problems, operational inefficiencies and conflict due to the nature of the job are also relevant.

Social attitudes stem from factors such as background, family influence, circle of friends, media influence and experiences to date. They are manifested in behaviours towards other people, for example political and prejudicial stances, exploitation of weaker groups, etc.

Management failings and social attitude problems, with regard to customer service, will manifest themselves in the form of things going wrong at the point of customer contact, such as face-to-face communications; the ability to listen and summarize; the manner and style of letter writing; telephone technique; and the handling of complaints.

Understanding, accepting and admitting the underlying reasons for customer service failures is half the battle. Shifting attitudes, many of which are deeply engrained, is not easy. This requires bold and active commitment, especially from the top, and will only be maintained through constant vigilance.

Within the framework of this activity your primary role is to facilitate discussion of these important issues. You also need to move participants towards suggesting ways in which attitudes may be changed and how they, as individuals, can influence the service they give and the service they receive.

1. After a brief introduction, divide participants into groups of four or five and distribute a copy of Document 29.1, Attitudes to service, to each participant. Ask groups to address each question and prepare to give feedback on their findings to the main group.

2. In the main group, arrange presentations and record key points on a flipchart or whiteboard. Discuss and allow sufficient time for questions.

3. Reform participants into their groups and ask them to consider the following questions which can be written up on a flipchart, again preparing themselves to give feedback to the main group:

    - How could you encourage positive attitude changes towards providing customer service in this organization? Specifically, what would you do?

- How could you, as individuals, influence the service that you receive from your suppliers? Specifically, what could you do?

Groups may wish to consider both 'internal' and 'external' supplier–customer chains. Alternatively, the internal and external focus could be shared between the different groups.

4. In the main group, ask groups to give feedback on their findings. Make sure that a full discussion on common ground and differences takes place, and ask participants to record points of agreement.

5. Allow time for participants to decide and write down *four* statements of what they intend to do differently as providers of service and as receivers of service (two statements for each role). Ask participants to announce their intentions publicly. Finally, review the learning from the activity.

## Time required

1. Completing Document 29.1 takes thirty to forty-five minutes.
2. Presentations and discussion take forty-five to fifty minutes.
3. Preparing answers to questions takes thirty to forty minutes.
4. Feedback, discussion and recording points take forty-five to fifty minutes.
5. Individual statements and review take thirty minutes.

Average total time: half a day, including breaks.

## Resources and materials needed

1. Sufficient copies of Document 29.1.
2. Sufficient space for participants to work undisturbed.
3. Flipchart or whiteboard, paper and pens.

*Document 29.1 (Page 1 of 2)*

# Attitudes to service

A complaint often heard is 'no one cares anymore.' The aim of this exercise is to discuss:

a)  Exactly *what* goes wrong?

and

b)  *why* does it go wrong?

You should investigate these two fundamental questions by discussing the following.

Please record your group's responses on a flipchart for subsequent presentation and discussion in the main group.

1. When customer service fails what specifically goes wrong? (Brainstorm if necessary)

2. The failures you have identified will generally stem from management controllable issues and/or social issues. Categorize these failures under the two headings:

    Management failings:                Social attitude problems:

*Reproduced from Facilitating Change: Ready-to-use training materials for the manager* by Barry Fletcher, Gower, Aldershot

*Document 29.1 (Page 2 of 2)*

3. Which deep-seated social attitudes affect your organization?

4. Which of these affect 'face-to-face' service, and how?

5. What are the *top five* causes of less than perfect service in your organization?

Reproduced from *Facilitating Change: Ready-to-use training materials for the manager*
by Barry Fletcher, Gower, Aldershot

# 30

# Improving customer care

*'Consider every customer to be a potentially lifelong customer, generating word-of-mouth referrals: ... the customer, in spirit and in flesh, must pervade the organization – every system in every department, every procedure, every measure, every meeting, every decision.'*
(Tom Peters, *Thriving on Chaos*, Pan/Macmillan, 1987)

All of us are customers for some of the time and therefore we know what it feels like to be a satisfied customer and a dissatisfied one. Within all of us lies the knowledge and understanding of what suppliers and providers can do to delight us and disappoint us. Some of us ponder on the contradiction that the people who disappoint us with poor service possess the knowledge and understanding to delight us!

This group activity encourages participants to draw on their wealth of experience as customers and to translate this into positive actions to delight the people they serve.

## Benefits

Participants undertaking this activity can expect to:

- sharpen their understanding about what constitutes customer care;
- produce a customer care programme based on their experience of unsatisfactory care;
- prepare their own customer care action plan.

*Facilitating Change*

## Suitable for

This activity is suitable for teams or groups wishing to:

- establish a customer care programme;

- respond to current problems, for example to criticisms from customers, complaints or declining performance;

- strive for continuous improvement of customer care arrangements.

## What to do

1. After a brief introduction encourage participants to contribute their views on 'What is customer care?' This can be achieved by brainstorming or group discussion.

2. Distribute a copy of Document 30.1, Customer care – chamber of horrors, to all participants, and ask them to complete it individually or in pairs.

3. Divide participants into groups of three or four and ask them to undertake the following tasks:

    (a) Individually relate their chosen incident, as described in Document 30.1, to the group.

    (b) Produce a consolidated list of the missing ingredients which lead to customer dissatisfaction.

4. In the main group, ask each group to give feedback on its findings. All lists can be displayed simultaneously or someone can speak on behalf of each group. Encourage discussion to identify common ground and work towards an agreed composite list of missing ingredients.

5. Ask groups to produce an outline customer care programme which would benefit the organization, department, team or other area of their choosing. Prompt them to consider both 'internal' and 'external' customers and to take account of the master list of missing ingredients agreed in Step 4. Ask each group to agree a method for presenting their outline programme to the main group.

6. Bring participants together and ask each group to carry out its presentation, allowing time for questions and discussion. Ask participants to record what they consider to be the *six* main points which emerge from the presentations.

*Improving customer care*

7. Distribute Document 30.2, Customer care – action plan, and ask each participant to complete it individually.

8. Encourage participants to share and comment on each other's plans and to agree ways in which they can work together and support each other in their achievement.

## Time required

1. Introduction and scene setting take ten minutes.
2. Completing Document 30.1 takes thirty minutes.
3. Sharing incidents and listing missing ingredients take thirty minutes.
4. Feeding back findings and agreeing composite list take twenty to thirty minutes.
5. Producing outline customer care programmes takes twenty to thirty minutes.
6. Presentations and recording six main points take forty to sixty minutes.
7. Completing Document 30.2 takes twenty minutes.
8. Sharing individual plans and seeking support take twenty to thirty minutes.

Average total time: four hours, including short breaks.

## Resources and materials needed

1. Sufficient copies of Documents 30.1 and 30.2.
2. Sufficient space for participants to work undisturbed.
3. Paper, pens, flipchart paper.
4. Video camera and playback facilities (optional).

Document 30.1 (Page 1 of 4)

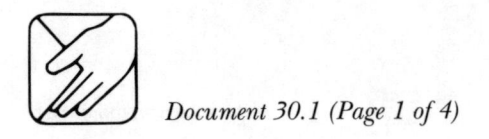

# Customer care – chamber of horrors

## Part 1

The following stories describe actual incidents. As you read through each account write down any missing ingredients which you believe led to customer dissatisfaction:

| Account of incident | Missing ingredient |
|---|---|
| **INCIDENT 1**<br>Mrs James was delighted with her new automatic washer/dryer – until it suddenly developed a leak one Sunday morning. It was only two weeks old and she was determined to call the service department first thing Monday morning.<br>  'A week on Tuesday?' shrieked Mrs James, 'but can't you make it sooner than that?'<br>  'Sorry Mrs James, but the engineers are very busy at the moment,' replied the service controller. 'If I can fit you in sooner I'll call you back,' she added.<br>  There was no call back and on the eve of the scheduled visit Mrs James rang to check the visit time. The same person responded, 'Sorry, but we can't say exactly when.'<br>  'Will it be morning or afternoon then?'<br>  'Sorry, the engineers are their own boss and they never tell us their movements,' replied the controller, quite indifferent to the fact that Mrs James had said she needed to visit the bank the next day.<br>  At 3.45 p.m. the engineer arrived, grumbling at having to climb the three flights of stairs with his bad back. He never looked Mrs James in the face, let alone the eye. She wondered if she was invisible.<br>  'Water is oozing from the door seal, my husband thinks it's a faulty seal' explained Mrs James. 'Knows about these things does he?' enquired the engineer sarcastically, while | |

Reproduced from *Facilitating Change: Ready-to-use training materials for the manager* by Barry Fletcher, Gower, Aldershot

| Account of incident | Missing ingredient |
|---|---|
| tugging and pulling on the rubber seal. 'It's the cotton fluff that collects between the seals,' called the engineer, sounding quite proud of his early diagnosis, 'you have to wipe these seals clean before every wash,' he added.<br>　'But surely it's not just that,' replied Mrs James, 'you see it's really oozing out.'<br>　'I suppose I'll just have to convince you then,' he grunted while setting the dial to the wash cycle.<br>　Both watched as the machine went through the critical parts of the cycle, speeded up by the short-cuts known only to the engineer. 'Nothing! You see it's the fluff, you must get rid of the fluff,' he admonished, pulling a report pad from his case. Mrs James made a telephone call while the engineer completed his report – slowly! She returned to hear a sharp crack, as if something had snapped. The engineer had his screwdriver prised behind the control dial.<br>　'I was curious', he explained. 'I thought the dial was out of position but it looks as if they've changed the design again.' He pressed the dial back into position and then left, rather hurriedly.<br>　Mrs James later recalled the incident to her husband. He thought is was quite funny and suggested, 'It's very difficult to find good staff these days.' A little later, his mood changed. He opened the washer door to load some washing and was drenched by water flooding from the machine. The engineer had forgotten to empty it!<br>　Cleaning up took an hour although some carpets were still very wet. Cautiously, Mr James tried again to load the machine, only to find that the control dial came off in his hand when turning it to set the cycle. A close look at the dial showed it to be broken.<br>　Next morning the service controller had a very irate customer on the line. 'Next Friday!' screeched the caller, 'let me tell you that if your | |

*Document 30.1 (Page 3 of 4)*

| Account of incident | Missing ingredient |
|---|---|
| engineer isn't here by this evening the machine will be in the garden for collection and you will be hearing from my solicitor!'<br><br>At 2.00 p.m. that afternoon a brand new, replacement machine was hauled up three flights of stairs. | |
| *INCIDENT 2*<br>The bus drew up alongside the queue of school children, splashing those too slow to jump back. It was a dark, wet, cold December night. Bobby held back until all the others were on the bus. The driver beckoned him to hurry. Bobby explained in a quiet whisper that he had lost his bus pass. The driver barked at him several times to speak up.<br><br>'Sorry lad, you know the rules: pass or cash and I don't care which!' exclaimed the driver, raising his voice for all the bus to hear. Bobby offered his name and address, but to no avail.<br><br>The bus pulled away, the other children pressing their faces against the windows and laughing at the lone thirteen-year-old beginning his three-mile trek home. | |

Reproduced from *Facilitating Change: Ready-to-use training materials for the manager*
by Barry Fletcher, Gower, Aldershot

*Document 30.1 (page 4 of 4)*

## Part 2

Now briefly describe an incident from your own experience which left you dissatisfied with the 'care' you received. As before, list the missing ingredients of customer care.

| Account of incident | Missing ingredients |
|---|---|
|  |  |

Reproduced from *Facilitating Change: Ready-to-use training materials for the manager*
by Barry Fletcher, Gower, Aldershot

*Document 30.2 (Page 1 of 2)*

# Customer care – action plan

1. Who are your customers (internal and external)?

2. How can you improve your level of care to each of them?

3. What specific actions will you need to take to achieve your suggestions at 2 above (also indicate when)?

Reproduced from *Facilitating Change: Ready-to-use training materials for the manager*
by Barry Fletcher, Gower, Aldershot

4. What are the potential benefits arising from your actions?

   a)  To your customers

   b)  To your organization, department or team

   c)  To you

# 31

# Increasing customer markets

A flexible, thought-provoking, group activity designed for the benefit of anyone who is involved in identifying and satisfying market needs. The activity examines markets currently being satisfied, together with providing time to reflect on current performance. Participants then explore possible avenues for increasing their markets and finally examine specific changes they wish to make.

## Benefits

Participants undertaking this activity can expect to:

- consider and draw conclusions about their current performance in terms of product*/service provision and markets served;
- explore the potential for increasing activity in each product and market sector;
- develop a strategy for change to which they are committed.

*Note: Where the word 'product' is used in this activity the word 'service' is equally applicable.

## Suitable for

This activity is suitable for a wide range of participants, indeed anyone who is supplying a product or service to others. Senior people could use the activity to inform their strategic decision-making process; that is, in considering the interplay between the organization and its 'external'

*Facilitating Change*

markets. Others, for example members of a team or department, can benefit from thinking about their local situation and opportunities which exist for satisfying and expanding 'internal markets' within the organization.

## What to do

You will need to be aware of the needs and expectations of participants. For participants addressing corporate and strategic issues, you can play an important part in getting them to consider the longer term, avoiding day-to-day details and distractions.

For those looking at more local and immediate issues, your skills can usefully be applied in helping participants to recognise and 'own' their situation, raising their understanding about their potential influence in bringing about change.

In all cases, you should encourage participants to detach themselves from early objections and barriers, concentrating more on the generation of creative ideas about new directions and alternatives open to them.

If the participants are interested in considering corporate and strategic issues you may wish to do some background reading. For example, *Corporate Strategy* by Igor H. Ansoff (Penguin, 1968) gives good basic information on the product/market matrix and life-cycle models. Your skills in facilitating the process are probably more valuable to the participants than your depth of knowledge of management subjects.

1. Briefly introduce the activity, explaining that its focus can be on 'internal' or 'external' markets. Through discussion, identify which market each participant would like to work on.

2. Divide participants into groups by placing participants together who have expressed a preference to work on one type of market. Distribute Document 31.1, Customer markets, and ask each group to complete the tasks described.

    *Note:* if working on 'internal' markets, groups may wish to use Document 26.2, Internal quality – evaluation form, suitably adapted, in place of (a) and (b) in Document 31.1.

3. Bring participants together and ask each group to make its presentation. Participants should raise questions and record key points and conclusions about the 'here and now' situation.

    *Note:* this step represents a starting point for considering alternative directions for increasing customer markets. One of the alternatives, covered in Step 4, is to provide more of the same products to current markets. Therefore, if current performance is judged to be less than satisfactory, improvements need to be made before proceeding.

*Increasing customer markets*

4. Distribute copies of Documents 31.2, Product/market matrix, and 31.3, The life cycle, to participants. Ask them to read the documents and then discuss and ask questions so that they understand the basic concepts, especially the relevance to both 'internal' and 'external' markets. Reform participants into their groups and ask them to complete the tasks outlined in Document 31.4, Considering alternatives.

    *Note:* depending on group composition there may be value in allocating different quadrants of the product/market matrix to different groups.

5. In the main group allow time for each group to present its findings. Encourage participants to ask questions, challenge each other, and offer constructive criticism and feedback.

6. Ask each group to work on a strategy for achieving its chosen alternative(s). Specific factors to consider include:

    - timing
    - responsibilities
    - resources
    - other people who need to be involved
    - specific actions and monitoring arrangements.

7. Back in the main group allow some time for sharing and discussing chosen strategies and encourage participants to comment on what work is still outstanding in the development of these strategies. Concentrate specifically on what the participants have learned from this activity.

## Time required

1. Introduction takes ten minutes.
2. Completing Document 31.1 takes fifty to sixty minutes.
3. Presentations and conclusions about the present situation take forty to fifty minutes.
4. Considering Documents 31.2 and 31.3 and completing Document 31.4 take sixty to ninety minutes.
5. The presentations take forty to fifty minutes.
6. Strategy development takes thirty to forty minutes.
7. Sharing and review take thirty to forty minutes.

Average total time: between a half and a full day, including breaks.

*Facilitating Change*

## Resources and materials needed

1. Sufficient copies of Documents 31.1, 31.2, 31.3, 31.4 and, if required, 26.2.

2. Sufficient space for participants to work undisturbed.

3. Paper, pens, flipchart paper.

4. Video camera and playback facilities (optional).

*Document 31.1 (Page 1 of 1)*

# Customer markets

Complete the following tasks:

(a) Clarify the 'here and now' situation for products and markets. Avoid becoming enmeshed in too much detail – think more in terms of 'product ranges' or 'groups of services' together with 'market or customer groups'. The main purpose here is to arrive at a clear *overview* of the present situation.

(b) Reach an objective assessment of current performance; that is, a judgement of how well you are performing with these products in these markets. A 1–10 rating scale may be helpful (1 = performing badly to 10 = excellent performance).

(c) Be prepared to present your key findings and any conclusions to the main group.

Reproduced from *Facilitating Change: Ready-to-use training materials for the manager*
by Barry Fletcher, Gower, Aldershot

*Document 31.2 (Page 1 of 1)*

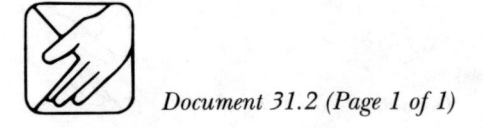

# Product/market matrix

|  | PRODUCTS/SERVICES | |
|---|---|---|
|  | Existing (here and now) | New |
| **MARKETS** Existing (here and now) | (a) Market penetration | (c) Product Development |
| New | (b) Market development | (d) Diversification |

*GROWTH STRATEGIES:*

**(a) Market penetration**

Involves a growth direction via the increase of market share for existing products in existing markets.

**(b) Market development**

Aims to seek new markets for existing products/services.

**(c) Product development**

Creates new products to supplement or replace current ones in existing markets.

**(d) Diversification**

Aims to supply new products/services to new markets.

Reproduced from *Facilitating Change: Ready-to-use training materials for the manager* by Barry Fletcher, Gower, Aldershot

*Document 31.3 (Page 1 of 1)*

# The life cycle (applied to products and markets)

The notion of the 'life cycle' can help you to take decisions about the interaction between your products or services and your markets (internal and external).

To illustrate, spend a few minutes considering the following combinations and their consequences for the supplier:

(a) a newly developing product supplied to a declining market;

(b) an established service supplied to a newly developing market;

(c) a growing market receiving a declining product;

(d) a mature product supplied to a declining market;

(e) a growing market receiving a newly developed service.

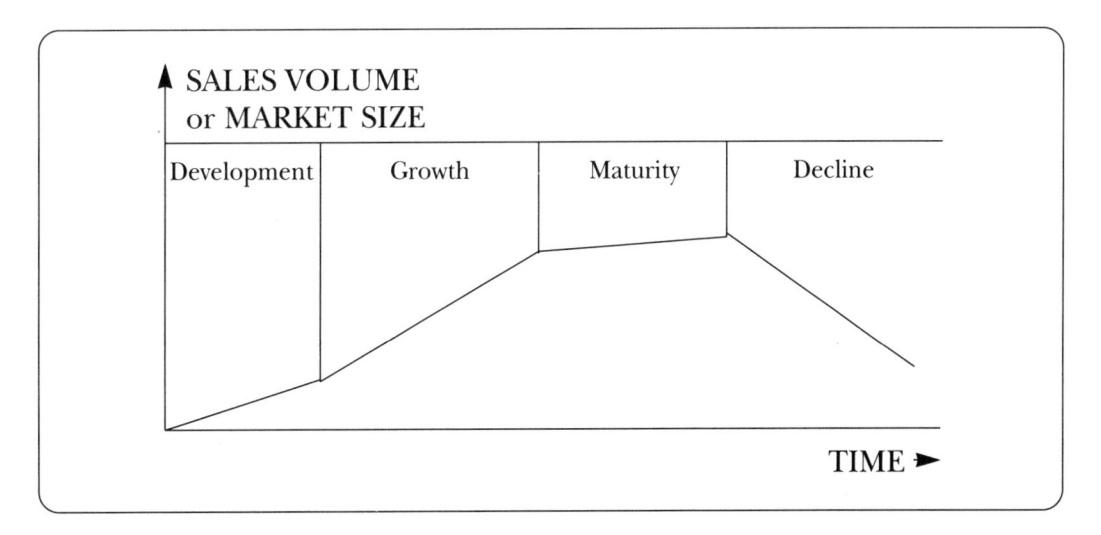

**Life cycle model for markets and products/services**

For detailed explanation and analysis of the interrelationships between life cycle users and buyers, suppliers and competitive conditions, consult *Exploring Corporate Strategy* by G. Johnson and K. Scholes, Prentice-Hall International, 1988.

*Document 31.4 (Page 1 of 1)*

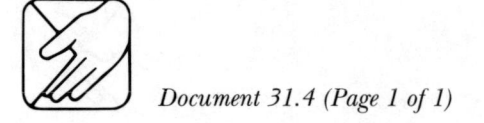

# Considering alternatives

Complete the following tasks:

(a) Consider the feasibility of increasing the level of activity (and thereby customer markets) within each quadrant of the product/market matrix.

(b) For each quadrant, specifically examine the implications for *skills, knowledge and perceived competence*.

(c) For each quadrant, draw conclusions about the effect of the life cycle (both for products and markets).

(d) Rank the four alternative strategies covered by the product/market matrix in order of preference for your situation.

(e) Prepare a presentation on the strategy you wish to implement, including your rationale, to be given to the main group.

# 32

# Empowering others

*It is impossible to empower others. They have to do it for themselves.*
Surely we can guide them?
*Nonsense. The key to empowering others is in accepting the need for authority – not authority in the traditional sense, but authority in a new sense meaning* **authorship.**
Really?
*The best we can do is to help others to write their story, to become authors in their own right.*

Are you regularly faced with situations where members of your staff enthusiastically offer proposals, suggestions, ideas, requests or hints about what they would like to happen? Are you inclined:

- to say 'Thanks, I'll think about it'
- to get involved in joint consideration of the details
- to say 'Yes, but ...'
- to say 'Let's think this through together, when we've got the time'
- to say 'Provided that you do it this way ...'
- to ask for a written supporting statement or cost–benefit analysis?

Have you thought of the effects which these, and similar responses, might have on the other person and their enthusiasm? And why are you inclined to respond in these ways?

This activity is designed to prepare you to respond in a different way – a way which will result in members of your staff feeling they have real authority for getting things done.

*Facilitating Change*

## Benefits

By undertaking this activity you can expect to:

- increase the chance that your staff will retain their desire to change things;
- enable your staff to hold onto their ownership of the change process;
- increase the extent to which your staff see you as their supporter.

## Suitable for

This activity is particularly useful to managers, supervisors, team leaders and directors.

## What to do

1. Compile a list of all the suggestions for change, explicit and implicit, that you have received from your staff during the recent past. Allow yourself plenty of time to think deeply about this, trying to remember hints, passing references and 'throw-away lines'.

2. Against each item on your list note the person's name and the response which you gave, if possible using your exact words.

3. Delete from the list *all* the suggestions which have been implemented.

4. Delete from the list those suggestions which, if implemented, would cause *serious harm* to the organization.

5. List all staff members whose names remain on your list. For each person ask yourself: 'Has this person a record of responsible behaviour in the organization?'

6. Arrange a meeting with each person for whom you answered 'yes' to the question in Step 5. Let them know you have thought about their suggestion, and say:

    *'You can pursue your suggestion in whatever way you choose.'*

## Time required

The time needed will vary according to the number of suggestions for change which you have noticed. It will also depend on how serious you are about empowering others. If you are committed to letting go you will complete this activity very quickly.

## Resources and materials needed

1. Time to think.
2. Writing materials.

# 33

# Providing a challenge

Challenges take many different forms. Confronting your boss, selling your house, organizing an expedition, speaking to strangers, crossing the road, parachuting, can all be construed as challenges. They also come to you from different sources – out of the blue, set by your partner, imposed by your boss and so on. All challenges share a common feature in that you can learn and develop from them, whether or not they are successfully met.

This learning potential is probably a good enough reason for you to set challenges for yourself. By providing yourself with a challenge you will be increasing your opportunities to learn something new; something which, once learned, can be used over and over again.

This activity is designed to motivate you to take on a challenge and to analyse the learning from it.

## Benefits

By undertaking this activity you can expect to:

- enjoy the process of setting yourself a challenge;
- achieve a detailed understanding of some challenging opportunities available to you;
- learn how ready you are to face a challenge now.

## Suitable for

This activity will be valuable to anyone who is interested in personal development and raising their self-awareness. Those who want to break new ground or develop an innovatory approach can also benefit.

*Facilitating Change*

## What to do

1. Make an appointment for a meeting with yourself and ensure you will not be interrupted. The first item on your agenda is to identify at least ten opportunities which you currently have to achieve something really worthwhile – for yourself, a colleague, a friend, your team, your organization or any cause you choose.

2. Now pick three of these opportunities, each of which attracts you for a different reason. Ensure as much variation as possible in your three choices.

3. For each choice produce a rich description of what your world would be like if you took the opportunity fully, invested a great deal of energy, and saw it through to a successful conclusion. It might help you to draw a picture, write a poem, list the benefits – the important thing is to imagine, from as many angles as possible, that it has happened.

4. Which of these detailed scenarios holds most appeal for you? Think carefully about the reasons for your choice and make a note of your conclusions.

5. You now have the prospect of providing yourself with a challenge.

   *Are you prepared to accept the challenge by committing yourself now to the pursuit of your desired result by a specific date?*

   The answer to this question will lead you to an action plan or to the realization that you are not yet ready to face a challenge.

## Time required

The time required will vary according to your current level of enthusiasm. However, you are challenged to complete all stages of the activity within one week.

## Resources and materials needed

1. Time to think.
2. Freedom from interruptions.
3. Writing and drawing materials.

# 34

# Taking a risk

How often do you see others doing things which you would like to do yourself but lack the courage to try? How often do you feel an inner disappointment, in work, social, family and leisure situations, arising from thoughts such as 'I wish I could do that' and 'if only I could pluck up the courage to try that' and 'I dare not try that'. Often there is a perceived risk which gets in the way of our fulfilling our wishes. It may be fear of embarrassment, fear of looking foolish, fear of getting it wrong or fear of failure. Interestingly, the people who are doing the things we would like to do appear not to be experiencing the same fears or perceiving the same risks.

This lively activity, designed for groups or teams but easily adapted for individual use, provides opportunities for participants to take a risk. The activity is designed to draw on the fact that different people perceive risk in different ways: what one person does as a matter of routine is perceived as risky by others.

## Benefits

Participants undertaking this activity can expect to:

- learn that risk is a matter of personal perception;
- learn that some of the things they do are perceived by others to be risky;
- decide to do, with support, something that has previously been seen as a risk.

*Facilitating Change*

## Suitable for

This activity is suitable for people who are interested in extending their repertoire of skills in dealing with situations containing an element of risk. It is particularly useful as an aid to team development because members can offer support and encouragement to each other when risks are being taken.

## What to do

As manager there is no reason why you cannot participate fully in this activity along with your team members; you can gain as much from it as anyone. While you may be tempted to maintain a work focus during the activity, a suggestion is for you to take the risk of being more open minded. Raising the willingness of participants to take risks is probably far more important than where they started to gain their extra confidence.

The activity can be presented in one session or as a continuing process spread over a number of regular meetings of your team. You may wish to prepare flipcharts in readiness for Steps 2, 3 and 4.

1. Introduce the activity as an opportunity to explore the subject of risk taking while learning a little more about each other and having some fun.

2. Encourage everyone to describe some of the things they do at work and away from work. For example, things that are:

    - challenging
    - fulfilling
    - practical
    - hair raising
    - satisfying
    - difficult
    - interesting
    - exciting
    - fun
    - dangerous
    - thought provoking
    - taxing
    - artistic
    - testing
    - stimulating
    - demanding
    - rewarding
    - new
    - exhilarating
    - unusual

    Questions and prompts will help to maintain the flow of information. While each person is speaking others should write down all the things that others do that they don't do, and have not done, themselves.

Explain that good-quality note taking at this stage is important for the next stages of the activity. Ensure that everyone is allowed time to contribute.

3. Allow time for participants to work individually to consider their lists and to divide the things that others do into the following two categories:

    - those things which I genuinely have no interest in doing myself;
    - those things which I have an interest, no matter how slight, in doing myself.

    Encourage participants to be honest with themselves in making this distinction; some may anticipate what is coming next and be tempted to express interest only in those things which do not have any risk attached. Supply coloured pens and highlighter pens as required for this task.

4. Give each participant a sheet of flipchart paper and suitable pens and explain the next task. This is to enter *all* those things in which interest has been expressed onto a 'risk line' as shown below, graded between 'no risk' and 'far too risky'.

    ```
    |─────────────────────────────────────────|
    no risk                            far too risky
    whatsoever                       to contemplate
    ```

5. Working in pairs, participants can next share what they have done so far and help each other to make a mark on their risk line which divides it into two parts, as shown below.

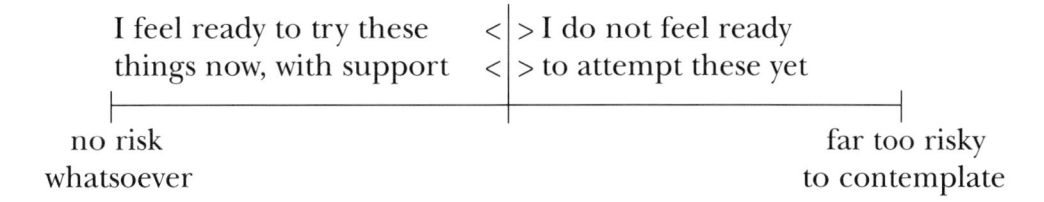

    ```
    I feel ready to try these      <|> I do not feel ready
    things now, with support       <|> to attempt these yet
    |─────────────────────┬───────────────────|
    no risk                            far too risky
    whatsoever                       to contemplate
    ```

    Partners can help each other to choose one thing from the left-hand side of the mark which they are now prepared to attempt. They can discuss each other's choices to check that there is a level of perceived risk and a degree of challenge.

6. Back in the main group, invite participants to describe their choices and to agree a plan of action with others. Aim for collaboration between *those who have done* and *those who haven't done*. This collaboration can take many forms, for example:

    - acting as a coach;

*Facilitating Change*

- acting as a consultant;
- providing the opportunity;
- accompanying the person who is taking the risk;
- offering psychological support and encouragement;
- observing the person taking the risk and giving feedback.

Encourage participants to describe their conclusions from the activity and what they have learned.

This concludes the formal part of the activity and people can proceed with the implementation of their plans. During subsequent team meetings you and your staff can discuss progress and share experiences, and results, of risk taking.

## Time required

1. The introduction takes five to ten minutes.
2. Individual contributions and note taking, allowing an average of fifteen minutes each, take two hours (based on a group of eight people).
3. Dividing the lists individually takes ten to twenty minutes.
4. Completing 'risk lines' individually takes ten to twenty minutes.
5. Working in pairs to choose a risk takes fifteen to twenty minutes.
6. Action planning to take risks and reviewing the learning take thirty to forty minutes.

Average total time: three hours and thirty minutes.

## Resources and materials needed

1. Pre-prepared flipcharts for Steps 2, 3 and 4.
2. A supply of flipchart paper, coloured pens, highlighter pens and marker pens.
3. Space in which to spread out and complete flipcharts.

# 35

# Welcoming the unknown

Most of us have doubts and fears about the unknown. This is healthy. Imagine standing on the edge of a precipice without feeling anxious. A few minutes' reflection will confirm that we have always lived with the unknown and found our own ways of greeting it. Becoming acquainted with how frequently and skilfully we have already responded to the unknown can help us to value the opportunities it brings.

This group activity is designed to help members to welcome their uncertain futures.

## Benefits

Participants undertaking this activity can expect to:

- raise their awareness of how they have previously coped with the unknown;
- recognize the unknown for what it is – both threat and opportunity;
- increase their confidence in facing the unknown;
- value the unknown for the potential it promises.

## Suitable for

This activity is especially useful for a team or group which is experiencing a higher than usual level of change, as in a merger, takeover or major reorganization. It will also benefit people who are interested in self-development and managing change.

*Facilitating Change*

## What to do

You are recommended to participate fully throughout this activity.

1. Brainstorm the question 'What does the unknown mean to you?', encouraging someone to record all the words used on a flipchart.

2. Explore the words to discover any patterns, contradictions and differences, for example:

   | positives | negatives |
   | threats | opportunities |
   | hopes | concerns. |

3. Form two groups, each with the task of:

    (a) identifying the full range of unknowns which have already been faced during group members' lives,

    and

    (b) highlighting any of these which did not have some positive result in the short or longer term.

4. In the main group share each other's findings and draw conclusions about similarities and common themes.

5. Encourage a group discussion of the question 'What is the value of the unknown?', the object of which is to produce an agreed group statement.

## Time required

1. Brainstorming takes ten to fifteen minutes.
2. Exploring the words for patterns takes fifteen minutes.
3. Work in small groups takes thirty to forty minutes.
4. Sharing findings and drawing conclusions takes ten to fifteen minutes.
5. Discussion and group statement take thirty to forty minutes.

Average time for activity: two hours including a short break.

## Resources and materials needed

1. Rooms for small groups to work.
2. Flipcharts, paper and pens.

# It's Not Luck

*A Gower Novel*

Eliyahu M Goldratt

Alex Rogo has had a great year, he was promoted to executive vice-president of UniCo with the responsibility for three recently acquired companies. His team of former and new associates is in place and the future looks secure and exciting. But then there is a shift of policy at the board level. Cash is needed and Alex's companies are to be put on the block. Alex faces a cruel dilemma. If he successfully completes the turnaround of his companies, they can be sold for the maximum return, but if he fails, the companies will be closed down. Either way, Alex and his team will be out of a job. It looks like a lose-lose situation. And as if he doesn't have enough to deal with, his two children have become teenagers!

As Alex grapples with problems at work and at home, we begin to understand the full scope of Eli Goldratt's powerful techniques, first presented in *The Goal*, the million copy best-seller that has already transformed management thinking throughout the Western world. *It's Not Luck* reveals more of the Thinking Processes, and moves beyond *The Goal* by showing how to apply them on a comprehensive scale.

This book will challenge you to change the way you think and prove to you that it's not luck that makes startling improvements achievable in your life.

# Gower

# New Leadership for Women and Men

## Building an Inclusive Organization

Michael Simmons

What are the key attributes of successful leaders in today's organization? The answer to this question is of course hotly debated. But Michael Simmons' ground-breaking book is the first to place the development of a new leadership for women and men at the heart of the argument. In particular, it is the first to focus on the benefits of helping leaders to overcome the negative effects of gender conditioning on the quality of their leadership.

The author proposes that leaders must transform their organizations by learning how to manage a turbulent environment, increase productivity and quality, and build an "inclusive organization". Achieving these aims requires that *everyone* is involved in planning the future direction of the enterprise and contributes to its continual improvement. But gender conditioning leads many managers to put up barriers to the full involvement of all their people. Transformation means reaching beyond equality to an organization where boundaries and limitations are not placed upon anyone. It needs a new kind of leadership capable of harnessing the intelligence, creativity and initiative of people at all levels, especially those who have traditionally been excluded.

This timely book provides much more than a searching analysis of women and men's leadership. Using real-life examples and case studies, it sets out strategies, programmes and techniques for improving organizational performance, and describes in detail the type of training needed. In short, it is a book designed to inspire not just thought but action.

# Gower

# The Practice of Empowerment

**Making the Most of Human Competence**

Dennis C Kinlaw

Organizations are downsizing, re-engineering and restructuring at an ever-increasing rate. The challenge now is to find better and better ways of harnessing the mental resources of the people who remain.

Dr Kinlaw, one of America's leading authorities on management development, sees empowerment as a way of improving organizational performance by making the most competent people the most influential most of the time, and his book provides a comprehensive and detailed model for achieving this objective. Drawing on examples and case studies from successful companies, Dr Kinlaw describes a practical, step-by-step process for introducing or extending empowerment in an organization or any part of an organization, and shows how to use feedback, team development and learning to good effect.

For managers considering, or involved in, empowerment programmes, and for concerned HR and training professionals, this new book represents an important resource for improving organizational performance.

Gower

# Process Improvement

**A Handbook for Managers**

Sarah Cook

Sarah Cook's latest book offers a systematic, customer-focused approach to improving the way we work. The methods it describes can be applied equally to a specific area or function and to the organization as a whole.

The author outlines a four-stage approach and shows what is involved at each stage and how to use the relevant techniques. The text is supplemented by case studies drawn from a variety of businesses and notes on sources of further information.

For managers, team leaders, trainers and consultants looking for practical ways to enhance organizational performance, here is a powerful new tool.

# Gower

# Professional Proposal Writing

Jane Fraser

What is the best way to structure a proposal? What style should it be written in? How can you demonstrate your capabilities to a potential client in writing? How do you distinguish your company from the competition?

These are some of the questions Jane Fraser addresses in this lively and practical guide. Based on the proposal-writing courses she runs for Oxford University, her book will help you to organize your ideas to maximum effect. She also suggests some standard formats for proposals and sales letters. Using entertaining real-life examples Dr Fraser provides simple rules for clear, reader-friendly writing and reveals the secrets of persuasive prose. Advice on layout, illustration, printing and binding is also here. Finally, she explains how to develop your proposal into a powerful presentation designed to win you new business.

The strength of a proposal can gain business or lose it. The stakes can often be high and the pressure to get it right intense. For sales and marketing people, managers, consultants, engineers and technical specialists of every kind, *Professional Proposal Writing* will be an invaluable aid to anyone who's struggled with proposals in the past or is faced with constructing them in the future.

# Gower

# Project Leadership

## 2nd Edition

Wendy Briner, Colin Hastings and Michael Geddes

The bestselling first edition of this book broke new ground by focusing on the leadership aspects of project management rather than the technical. This radically revised edition is substantially reorganized, to introduce much new material and experience and bring the applications up to date.

Project leaders now exist in many different types of organizations, and they and their projects extend far wider than the construction work where traditional project management began. This new edition begins by explaining why the project way of working has been so widely and enthusiastically adopted, and provides new material on the role and key competences of project leaders in a wide range of different organizations. The authors provide invaluable guidance to senior managers struggling to create the context within which project work can thrive as well as be controlled. A new section, 'Preparing the Ground' reflects their increased emphasis on getting projects off to the right start, with new insights into the scoping process designed to ensure all parties agree on objectives. It also demonstrates the importance of understanding the organizational and political factors involved if the project is to succeed in business terms.

Part III shows how to handle the issues that arise at each stage of the project's life including a whole new section on the critical process of project team start up. The final section contains a thought-provoking "action summary" and a guide to further sources of information and development.

Project leadership and the project way of working has moved on. This book will provide both a conceptual framework and a set of practical tools for all those who find themselves permanently or occasionally in the project leader role, as well as an invaluable guide to setting up and maintaining project activity.

# Gower

# Re-Engineering at Work

Michael Loh

Business process re-engineering, in various forms and under various names, continues to sweep through the organizational world. "It has to be done", says Peter Drucker. Yet many re-engineering programmes are falling short of expectations, or failing altogether. In most cases, according to Dr Loh, this is because insufficient attention has been paid to the human element.

Changing an organization means changing the behaviour of its people. And unless those people are enthusiastic no lasting change will take place. Dr Loh sets out a simple four-stage framework for introducing a re-engineering programme. Using examples drawn from a wide range of organizations in many different cultures, he explains what is involved at each stage and shows how to align the aspirations of the individual with the goals and visions of the organization. Only in this way can you secure genuine commitment and minimize resistance to change. And only in this way can you ensure that any improved performance will be sustained.

Lively in style and eminently practical, *Re-Engineering at Work* is necessary reading for anyone involved in transforming an organization.

# Gower

# Structured Problem Solving

*A PARSEC Guide*

Graham W Parker

Problems represent the difference between where we are now and where we want to be - obstacles in the journey to our goals. They erode our ability to compete, they prevent our success and they undermine our morale. Successful organizations, though, regard a problem as an opportunity for improvement - for learning a lesson that can be put to profitable use. In such organizations identifying and eliminating problems has become a way of life.

This book provides a systematic approach to solving business problems, designed to maximize the likelihood of finding the optimum solution in each case. Part I outlines the process involved. Part II describes and illustrates no fewer than 33 problem-solving "tools" and includes a grid that enables their respective uses and merits to be compared at a glance.

Managers and other professionals will find this PARSEC Guide a powerful aid to more effective performance.

# Gower

# Teambuilding Strategy

Mike Woodcock and Dave Francis

There is no doubt that working through teams can be an effective way to accomplish tasks in an organization. As Mike Woodcock and Dave Francis point out, though, it is by no means the only one. Managers concerned with human resource strategy cannot afford to assume that teamwork will always be the best option. A number of questions need to be asked before any decision is made.

Among these questions are the following • what should be the focus of our organization development interventions? • should we undertake teambuilding initiatives? • how extensive should the teambuilding initiative be? • what resources will we need to support our teambuilding initiative?

This book provides a framework within which these questions may be addressed. It presents a structured approach to analysing the key issues, including a series of questionnaires and activities designed to guide the reader through the key strategic decision that must be taken by any organization contemplating a teambuilding programme. The authors, two of the best known specialists in the field, examine the benefits and dangers of teambuilding as an organization development strategy and offer detailed guidance on further information and resources.

This is the second and considerably reworked edition of *Organization Development Through Teambuilding*, first published in 1982.

Gower

# The Truth About Outsourcing

Brian Rothery and Ian Robertson

Outsourcing is undoubtedly one of the most important developments of recent years in the way organizations are managed. The scale of the movement - and the range of functions involved - has grown immeasurably in recent years and is increasing at a remarkable rate. Yet confusion and misunderstanding still surround it.

This timely book charts the rise and rise of the outsourcing phenomenon in business and the public sector.
The authors examine both the "why" and the "how" and describe the experience of numerous organizations which have taken the outsourcing route. They examine the advantages, the possibilities and the pitfalls. Which activities lend themselves to contracting out? Which never should be? What are the criteria for deciding? How do you select suitable subcontractors - and control them? These and many other questions are addressed with the aid of real-life case studies. The tone is practical throughout, and the book contains detailed guidance on legal and personnel aspects of the subject, including a model contract and a methodology for evaluating an outsourcing proposal.

No organization should embark on a programme of outsourcing without a careful study of this book.

Gower

# The Turbocharged Company

**Igniting Your Business to Soar Ahead of the Competition**

Larry Goddard and David Brown

Imagine, for a moment, that the business you own or work for is so successful that you cannot wait to get there each day. Sales are better than planned, and costs are on the decrease; the company's making money in a competitive marketplace, whilst providing exceptional value to your customers. All staff are productive and dedicated; customers write to applaud your service, not to complain.

Sounds too good to be true? But what if it could be a reality for your organization?

Goddard and Brown set out to find out how a handful of US companies stood head and shoulders above the rest. They looked at nearly 1,000 of the largest US businesses, and identified just 3% that they described as 'turbocharged' - all had outperformed their closest competitor by more than 40% over three years. All had somehow turned a level playing field into a significant competitive advantage. But how? On the face of it, they subscribed to a wide range of different business philosophies.

In this book, the authors identify the common factors - the 'turbocharged process' that put these companies out of the reach of their rivals. This total approach to business success incorporates a range of strategies such as TQM, ISO 9000, Benchmarking and Statistical Process Control (SPC), but is based on four essential foundations:

- unleashing people power
- Not just listening to, but revering your customers
- relentlessly pursuing productivity
- focusing on strengths, and on being the leader in your field.

Packed with examples from America's turbocharged companies, this book will help you build these foundations and get ahead of your competitors.

# Gower

Ministry of Education & Training
MET Library
13th Floor, Mowat Block, Queen's Park

SEP 24 1997